THE SECOND
INDOCHINA WAR

AMONG OTHER BOOKS BY THE SAME AUTHOR

Again Korea, 1968
Vietnam North, 1966
Vietnam: Inside Story of the Guerrilla War, 1965
The Furtive War: The United States in Vietnam and Laos, 1963
Mekong Upstream, 1959
China's Feet Unbound, 1952
Bombs Over Burma, 1944

The Second Indochina War

Cambodia and Laos

by **WILFRED G. BURCHETT**

INTERNATIONAL PUBLISHERS
New York

959.7
B 94s

SBN (hardback) 7178-0307-4; (paperback) 7178-0308-2
Manufactured in the United States of America

Contents

Introduction

When, on April 30, 1970 American troops and tanks rumbled across the South Vietnamese frontier into neutral Cambodia, the second Indochina war started. There was no longer a separate ground war in South Vietnam, an air war in North Vietnam, a "secret war" in Laos. They had been fused into a single front as existed sixteen and more years previously until the 1954 Geneva Agreements put an end to France's Indochina war. Despite all that has been said about "limited objectives" and deadlines for U.S. troop withdrawals, future historians will fix April 30, 1970 as the start of the second war of Indochina. From then on, just as there would be one single war, there could be only one single peace, an Indochina peace—providing the conflict can be limited to the states now involved.

A week before the invasion was launched, U.S. Secretary of State William P. Rogers had assured a Congressional Appropriations Committee that no American troops would be sent to Cambodia. A few days after it started, President Nixon and Secretary for Defense Melvin R. Laird gave assurances that the invasion was limited in time and space—two months and a depth of some 20 miles inside Cambodia.

Within a couple of weeks, a flotilla of gunboats, with an umbrella of U.S. planes and helicopters, moved up the Mekong river, a hundred or so miles into Cambodia. The Saigon leaders, with U.S. blessing, were stating that their troops had gone to Cambodia to stay. Gunboats on the Mekong! It smelt strongly of the most rapacious phase of 19th century colonialism. "Is anybody sure what that flotilla of South Vietnamese gunboats is doing on the Mekong River?" the Washington *Post* asked editorially on May 13. After examining the dubious official pretexts for this action, the paper asked: "Where there are gunboats, can some kind of gunboat diplomacy be far behind?"

The expedition up the Mekong was in fact a logical, if startling, extension of the U.S. military-political invention of "special war" which had its first tryout in South Vietnam from the end of 1961 onward. Perhaps later this form of war will be recogized as the classic example of the application of the often ill-defined and much misunderstood term "neo-colonialism," in its up-to-date version. It is "special war" in the era of "Asiatization," a teleguided form of U.S. colonization of Asia—the practical content of the old John Foster Dulles concept of "Let Asians fight Asians" where that suits U.S. interests.

"Special war" was one of the three types of war which the late President Kennedy's advisers including Henry Kissinger, now President Nixon's adviser on national security affairs, persuaded him the United States must prepare to fight. The great thing about "special war" was that others did the fighting while the United States put up the dollars and arms, provided strategic and tactical direction through a corps of U.S. "military advisers," and support facilities such as air power and air transport—everything in fact except the cannon fodder. Among the advantages of "special war" was that it was run on the cheap. As one enthusiastic advocate said at a session of the Congressional Armed Services Committee, after explaining the fractional cost of maintaining a local soldier as compared to an American: "And when they die, you don't have to ship them home. You bury them right there on the spot." An equivalent of U.S. Ambassador Ellsworth Bunker's remark in favor of the Nixon policy of "Vietnamization": "It's a question of changing the color of the corpses."

"Special war" failed in Vietnam and had to be moved up to the next stage of "local" or "limited" war, in which American combat troops are involved, but which is limited in scope and stops far short of the third and last "global, nuclear" war. "Special war" has been waged by the United States in Laos since late 1960, as explained in the chapters that follow. From April 1970 it has been waged in Cambodia.

The South Vietnamese invasion of Cambodia backed by U.S. power took the concept a step further. Instead of U.S.-supported local forces employed to maintain a pro-U.S. regime in power in their own country, they were now sent to invade a neighboring country for the same purpose. An obvious advantage was that the action could be shrugged off as "South Vietnamese"—not bound by any of the rules Washington pretended it was imposing on its own military commanders.

The purpose of this book is to show that what is happening in Cambodia and Laos today has nothing to do with "Sihanouk trails," "Ho Chi Minh trails" or "Vietcong sanctuaries or bases" but represents a logical extension of policies followed by the United States in the area since 1954—policies deliberately planned to "fill the power vacuum" created by the collapse of French colonialism in Indochina. It is as simple as that; all the rest is decoration and juggling with semantics.

Washington deliberately set out to wreck the 1954 Geneva Agreements which it refused to sign but pledged to respect. In refusing to accept the elections to unify Vietnam—to have been held in July 1956 according to the Geneva Agreements—in refusing to respect the neutrality of Laos and Cambodia and consistently working to overthrow truly neutralist regimes in those countries, U.S. policy-makers created step by step the grave situation which exists in the former states of Indochina today. The concept of Laos and Cambodia as neutral buffer states was the basis for the meeting of East-West minds at the 1954 Geneva Conference. Specifically it was the meeting of minds between Anthony Eden and Pierre Mendes-France on the one side and of Chou En-lai and Vyacheslav Molotov on the other, to which the states immediately concerned agreed. But Dulles stalked out of the Geneva Conference and later denounced neutrality as "dangerous and immoral."

The end result is a second Indochina war. Typical of the newest development of neo-colonialism is the flotilla on the Mekong, consisting of puppet gunboats. Also typical is the cooperation of Thai and South Vietnamese puppets with Cambodia sub-puppets to try and tear Cambodia to bits and transform it into a sub-colony. The entire course of the escalation of American intervention in its various forms has been witnessed by the author as an on-the-spot reporter of the unfolding drama of Indochina from the beginnings of the battle of Dien Bien Phu and the 1954 Geneva Conference to the formation of a Royal Cambodian Government of National Union in Peking on May 5, 1970.

When the CIA brought about the downfall of Prince Norodom Sihanouk of Cambodia and his neutralist concepts, they started a chain reaction of events, the ultimate consequences of which are unpredictable. Not only did they bring the Vietnam war onto Cambodian soil within a matter of days and create a single warfront in all Indochina. In blowing up the restraining dam of Cambodian neutrality U.S. policymakers have started a "no-frontiers" war which might well blaze its way across all of southern Asia to the gates of India and beyond.

Washington has made much of "Communist sanctuaries" in Cambodia. There are far more important American "sanctuaries" in Thailand; here also are important guerrilla bases stretching across to the frontiers with Malaysia. And despite the claims made about Sir Robert Thompson as the "victor of counter-insurgency" in Malaya, there is still an incipient, unfinished guerrilla war there. The hard core and leadership of the Malayan guerrillas, whom Sir Robert never defeated militarily, remains intact and active in the Thailand-Malaysia frontier area. The extension of "special war" in Laos, by May 1970 had brought about a linkup in north-western Laos between Pathet Lao guerrillas with those of the Thailand Patriotic Front who in that area are mainly of Laotian ethnic origin.

Had the Vietnam war been confined within the frontiers of Vietnam, had it been settled along lines that started to be defined at the Paris talks, other problems would have remained isolated and would have developed at a tempo corresponding to the economic and social levels of the countries concerned. President Nixon decided on "Viet-namizing" the war instead of ending it, on expanding it instead of limiting it. American intervention—and in some cases, as with Thailand and the Philippines—merely the American presence acts as a powerful fertilizer on embryo resistance movements. And they will not just fade away because of gunboats up the Mekong. This is a hard fact of the 1970's with which President Nixon and his successor will have to reckon.

Paris   W.G. Burchett
June 1, 1970

Part I
Cambodia

1

Cambodia and its Place in Indochina

Fate allotted the states of Indochina a tragically unenviable role in the geopolitical order of things: A transit route and staging ground for invaders of other parts of Asia; a crossroads of rival imperialisms; a battleground for would-be conquerors of Indochina for its own attractions; a source of endless wars between the component states themselves trying to assert dominance over each other; a focal point for clashing cultures and religions. Too often has it been a veritable maelstrom of strife on the Asian mainland. Whether it was the armies of successive dynasties of feudal China or the Mongol Hordes moving South, western colonialists moving East, Japanese expansionists moving West in World War II, the United States aiming north at People's China—it was through Indochina that they passed and pitched their tents for years, decades and even centuries. Incredibly the peoples of Indochina have always resisted, often enough with arms in hand.

Why the name Indochina? The cultures and influences of India and China met on the peninsula in which today's Vietnam, Cambodia and Laos are situated. In this wider cultural context the term Indochina applies to all those states in the peninsula which starts on the eastern borders of today's East Pakistan. It includes Burma, Malaya, Thailand and the three states of former French Indochina, all of which were subject to a greater or lesser degree to the influences of India and China. For the purposes of the present book the term Indochina is used in the usual and narrower context as the area formed by Vietnam, Cambodia and Laos.

Vietnam, separated by the Annamite chain of mountains from Laos and Cambodia, was more strongly influenced by Chinese culture, partly because of centuries of Chinese occupation. Cambodia and Laos were at one time strongly influenced by Indian culture. The magnificent temples of Angkor in Cambodia bear witness to the struggle and sometimes the peaceful coexistence of the Hindu and Buddhist religions. The Vietnamese also adopted Buddhism, but a different variety than that of the two neighboring states, and at times tinged with Taoism.

Each of the three states has retained its distinctive culture; its language, way of dress and eating. The Vietnamese have adopted a Latin script for their written language while in Cambodia and Laos it is based on Sanskrit. Vietnamese, like Chinese and Koreans, eat with chopsticks, Cambodians with spoons and Laotians, like Indians, with their hands. The types of food they eat are different. Vietnamese food is similar to, but not identical with, Chinese. The Cambodians favor Indian-type curry and meat and fish cooked on a skewer. Laotian food is somewhere in between but the diet also includes raw meat. They are all rice-eaters, the Laotians tending to favor glutinous rice. The mountain-dwellers in all three countries favor maize and also glutinous rice as the staple diet. Each has retained its customs despite centuries of foreign occupation, having resisted absorption by the invaders.

Nature and climate have left a strong imprint on the character of the component states of Indochina. The level of political, social and economic development in each is quite different. To a certain extent this difference is also true as between North and South Vietnam, although language and customs are the same, with slight differences of accent, throughout the length and breadth of the country, for the Vietnamese proper. In the North the climate is relatively harsh, with great pressure of population on the cultivable land. Before the land reform which followed the French withdrawal after the 1954 Geneva Agreements, the land was in the hands of landlords who lived in the same village as the peasants and disputed every kilogram of rice wrested in the form of rent from the tenant farmers. In the South where nature is more generous, there was less pressure of population on the land. Landlords tended to live in the cities and dabble in trade, leaving agents to collect the rents. Many adopted French nationality; they sent their sons to study in France and behaved rather like European-type absentee landlords.

In Cambodia, with practically no pressure of population on the land, there is no traditional landlord system—only small farmers who own the land they till. But they often do not really own the crops they grow, having mortgaged them in advance to moneylenders or merchants who buy their crops cheap and sell them commodities dear. In Laos also there were no landlords, but in many parts of the country a sort of feudal system existed under which the *tasseng*, or appointed head of a group of villages, could call on the peasants to provide unpaid labor to till the local notables' land or other such work—sometimes up to six or eight months a year—and to surrender the choicest portions of the catch from fishing and hunting.

Among the Indochinese states—after the 1954 Geneva Agreements temporarily cut Vietnam in two at the 17th parallel—Laos is the biggest in terms of area, with 88,780 square miles. Cambodia comes next with 71,000 square miles then South Vietnam with 66,263 and North Vietnam with 63,344 square miles. In terms of population, however, Laos is by far the smallest with a total perhaps of three million, followed by Cambodia with about six million, both taken together overshadowed population-wise by North Vietnam with 17 million and by South Vietnam with 15 million. On the map, Indochina sticks out like a southern appendage of mainland China, as does Korea far away in the Northeast.

In contrast to the easy-going Cambodians and Laotians, the Vietnamese are energetic with great capacities for organization, discipline and hard work. The French used Vietnamese to staff their administrative machinery throughout Indochina, which caused many hard feelings against them. Vietnamese also established themselves as craftsmen and technicians in Cambodia and Laos and shared with Chinese the functions of merchants in the towns. Money in the sense of currency was introduced in Laos and Cambodia much later than in Vietnam and barter instead of money exchange is still very common in both countries. The Vietnamese also settled in as rice-growers and fishermen.

The Cambodian people, like the Laotian—until recent industrial development in Cambodia—lived mainly on the direct fruits of their labor, the rice they grew, the fish they caught, the game they hunted, the tools and weapons they forged, the cloth they wove. Their's was a subsistence and not a commodity economy. One of the most interesting events of the year in Cambodia is after the rice harvest when the peasant oxcart convoys rumble along the roads to the banks of the Tonle-Sap river, near Phnom Penh, where they barter their rice for a special type of fish, transformed on the spot into *prahoc*, a highly salted fish paste which provides a vitamin-rich element in the Cambodian diet. The lack of a commodity economy did not prevent the Cambodians from creating a highly developed civilization, as the ruins of the Angkor temples testify.

To study Cambodia's past, one must visit Angkor. There is little to prepare one for the first impact of the ancient capital and its ruins. One has read about them, seen photos and heard tales of their wonders. But nothing prepares the emotions for that first glimpse of the towers of Angkor Wat, rising like lotus buds above the jungle tops and mirrored in the waters of the surrounding moat. They are but the prelude to the gradual unfolding of the treasures of this, the most famous of the Angkor group of monuments. Angkor Wat itself is but one of at least a dozen other monuments of supreme historic and cultural importance in that great complex of buildings known as Angkor. Additional scores of fragments of lesser interest, except to the specialists, cover hundreds of acres.

Cambodia itself is a museum of ancient ruins, with over one thousand officially classified. But it is at Angkor, for half a millenium the capital of the Khmer kings, that the greatest concentration is found. If it is only the ruins of temples that today testify to the greatness of the ancient Cambodian architects and builders, this is because only the deities were considered worthy of buildings of stone. Mere mortals, even kings, were housed in wood at best, more often in bamboo and thatch. Because of this, the houses and palaces of the Golden Age of Cambodia disappeared without a trace—except as portrayed in the sculpted friezes of Angkor.

The first capital of what roughly corresponds to present-day Cambodia was established at Angkor, a few miles from the present-day town of Siem Reap, at the beginning of the ninth century. The pre-Angkorian history of Cambodia is not very exactly known. The best sources are Sanskrit inscriptions found at Angkor and first translated by Indian scholars, the Chinese Annals and accounts by Chinese travelers who visited the country from time to time. But historians generally are agreed that between the first and sixth centuries of our era there was a Hindu kingdom in what is now southern Cambodia. It was known as Fou-Nan by the Chinese. In the northern part lived a race known as the Kambujas, who were apparently vassals of the Kingdom of Fou-Nan. In the middle of the sixth century, the governor of the Kambujas declared himself independent of Fou-Nan and with the help of his brother set up a rival dynasty. Within a century the successors of the two brothers annexed the South and replaced the Kingdom of Fou-Nan by that of the Kambujas. For a period there were civil wars and the country was divided, part of it falling under the sovereignty of Java. Toward the end of the eighth century, a prince of the former ruling dynasty, who had been taken as a prisoner to Java, returned and reestablished the Kingdom of Kambuja with himself on the throne as King Jayavarman II. He declared independence from Java and established the first capital of a unified Cambodia near Angkor in what is today the province of Siem Reap.*

*The above account is summarized from various works by one of the best known French authorities on early Cambodian history, G. Goedes, including *Les capitales de Jayavarman II, La Tradition généalogique de Premier Rois d'Angkor* and *Pour mieux comprendre Angkor.*

Successive kings maintained their capitals in the same region until the mid-15th century when the western provinces were threatened by Siam. The ruins which today attract visitors from all over the world date from the beginning of the ninth to the end of the 13th centuries. Angkor Wat itself was built during the reign of King Suryavarman II (1112-82).

Jayavarman had brought with him from Java the theory of a god-king, or Devaraja (which has its counterpart in the "divine rights" so beloved of European monarchs in more recent times). He was, he claimed, an incarnation of Vishnu, Hindu Lord of the Universe, descended on earth. When he died, he would return to Mount Meru in his original form of Vishnu. The central tower of Angkor Wat represented Mount Meru and sheltered a *linnga* phallic symbol representing the king-god. The successors of Jayavarman II perpetuated this belief and each was obliged to construct, a "mountain temple" as residences for the royal *linnga*.

Prince Norodom Sihanouk is a spiritual descendant of the Angkor kings and the king-god theory is widely accepted by today's Cambodian peasantry. This reverence for the monarch has also a very earthly reason. The Angkor kings were first-class engineers and when one died, it was the best among the royal engineers who was elected the new king. Cambodian prosperity depended on water conservation. Unlike Vietnam, whose agriculture relied on the controlled flooding of the fields in the vast deltas of the Red river and the Mekong, Cambodian agriculture depended on man-made reservoirs and irrigation channels, around which the population tended to concentrate. Some modern Cambodian scholars, supported by French researchers, believe that the magnificence of Angkor is explicable because of the huge concentration of population around the excellent reservoirs and irrigation systems built by the Angkor kings, some of which still exist today. Angkor Thom, the main capital, is claimed to have been the biggest city in the world at the time of its greatest glory, with over a million inhabitants.

Gradually the reservoirs are believed to have become silted up, and centers of agriculture became dispersed nearer to the

Mekong and Bassac rivers. The theory is advanced that the network of roads, built by the last of the Angkor kings, Jayavarman VII, with inns spaced every eight to ten miles—an easy day's march—and well-equipped hospitals at regular intervals, were necessary for the transport of rice from various parts of the country to feed Angkor at a time when silted up irrigation systems had greatly reduced rice production in that area. Be that as it may, there is no doubt that the prosperity of the people depended on the skill, energy and organizational capacity of their engineer-kings, not to mention their military abilities.

One of the most important national holidays in present-day Cambodia is associated with the Plowing of the First Furrow, performed until his overthrow by Prince Sihanouk, with Brahman priests in attendance, a relic of the old days when Hinduism was the official religion.

Favorite themes in the sculptured galleries at Angkor Wat are from the Hindu epics, the Ramayana and Mahabharata. One can spend weeks examining these legends in stone, carved with zest and humor, the humanism and realism of the sculptors expressed in every chisel cut. But the artists' mood change when they portray battle scenes between Cambodians and Chams.*

Battle scenes are not shown in glamorized, heroic form but realistically, with all the horror and suffering that war brings. There is no glorification of even military successes. Cambodian troops are shown marching over a battlefield thick with their own dead. In the naval battles which took place on the Great Lake between multi-oared galleys laden with opposing troops—the Chams always recognizable by lotus-shaped headdresses—one sees the wounded toppling over-

*The empire of Champha was centered in what is now South Vietnam. Cambodia was repeatedly subject to Cham invasions, mostly by fleets sailing up the lower Mekong and attacking Angkor via the Great Lake which covers about 9,000 sq. kms. at the height of the rainy season. Later the Champha empire was destroyed by the Annamites and only a few thousand Chams now survive, a minority people scattered in isolated villages in South Vietnam and Cambodia.

board to be seized by crocodiles. The lake bottom is piled high with bodies, Cambodian and Cham, intertwined in death, prey for giant turtles, crocodiles and huge fish. The land battles are directed by generals on elephants armed with javelins, while the infantry fight with pikes and crossbows. Grim scenes show the fate of Cambodians taken prisoner, hung by the wrists on racks while spikes are driven into their bodies, then thrown into the flames their bodies still bristling with spikes.

Together with frescoes of war scenes are others (especially at the Bayon temple) portraying people building houses, bargaining at the market, hunting in the jungle with crossbows, fishing with nets, attending feasts, tilling the soil, watching cock fights and combats between wild boars—scores of scenes giving intimate glimpses of the life of the people as it then was and still is in many parts of the country today.

After Jayavarman VII, there was no further building of importance. Successive armies of Chams and Siamese swept back and forth, looting and burning. In 1297 the Chinese traveler, Chou Ta-kuan, found court life in Angkor still sumptuous but the country devastated and impoverished by wars with the Siamese. In 1432, Angkor was definitely abandoned as capital of the kingdom. The Siamese occupied it for a short time, but finally they also withdrew from what had become a pile of ruins. Most of the peasantry moved out of the Angkor region after the invaders destroyed a compli-cated irrigation system built at the same time as Angkor Wat. The jungle reclaimed the area; it became the home of herds of elephants, tigers and panthers. A splendid civilization fell into decay. Later generations of Khmers gazed in awe at the massive ruins and invented legends as to their origin.

In the early 17th century a Spanish missionary stumbled across the strange ruins—and concluded they had been built by the Romans or Alexander the Great!

It was not until the French seizure of Cambodia in 1862 that any serious study was made of them and the history of the 500 years of the Angkorian period was gradually pieced together.

2

Liberation from France

The modern history of Cambodia starts with French colonization. This was presaged with the arrival of French warships in Vietnam in 1858, ostensibly to "protect" French missionaries in Tourane (Danang) and Saigon. After Vietnam, Cambodia was next as France pieced together her Indochina colony. It is not the purpose of this book to deal with the details of French rule or the resistance of the Cambodian people to it, but certain elements of the resistance struggle and the role of Sihanouk in recovering the country's independence are essential to understand what is happening in Cambodia after the coup by Lon Nol and Sirik Matak in March 1970.

When the Japanese took over Indochina in December 1941, they were content in Cambodia as elsewhere to let the Vichy France administration continue to run civilian affairs. But on March 9, 1945, by which time the Vichy regime no longer existed, the Japanese staged a coup and took over completely. As in Vietnam and Laos, in August 1945 there was a popular uprising against the Japanese and state power was seized by patriotic resistance forces. But not for long. Supported by British warships and troops under Brig. General Gracey, French troops landed in Saigon on September 23, 1945, and after the resistance forces in Saigon were forced out of the capital the French used it as a base to move into Cambodia. On October 5, General Leclerc parachuted troops into Phnom Penh, thus officially opening the second French invasion of Cambodia—and thus began a new phase in the resistance struggle of the Cambodian people.

It is important to note that the French fought the war in

Indochina as a whole. In their original conquest they had used a foothold in South Vietnam to take Cambodia. From bases in Cambodia they had occupied the rest of South Vietnam. They used bases in Cambodia and Vietnam to seize Laos. In their reconquest in 1945 they used Saigon to move back into Cambodia and then used Cambodia to outflank the Vietnamese resistance forces in west and southwest Vietnam. For the outflanking movement designed to wipe out the Vietminh liberation forces in northern Vietnam, the French used Laos as their base. Fronts and battle areas overlapped from Vietnam to Laos, from Laos to Cambodia and from there back to Vietnam.

Because of the stiff resistance from the Vietminh in South Vietnam and the necessity to play for time to build up strength for the invasion of the North, promises were made to Cambodia, in a *modus vivendi* signed on January 7, 1946, of full independence "in principle." It was to be followed by treaties which would abolish the protectorate and cancel out the odious conventions extracted at pistol and bayonet-point at the end of the 19th century. But discussion on the treaties was always postponed while troops continued to arrive, and the French hold on the country tightened rather than loosened. The machine for recapturing Indochina was perfected and in December 1946, all-out war was launched against the people of Vietnam with the shelling of Haiphong and invasion of the Red River delta. With each French advance in Vietnam prospects for the implementation of the *modus vivendi* in Cambodia receded.

Reference to this situation and to the strength of the Khmer Issarak resistance movement was contained in a statement by Sam Sary,* at that time Minister for Conferences charged with negotiations with the French government. In complaining of the delays in granting full independence, nearly eight years after the *modus vivendi* had been signed, he pointed out: "This hesitant policy of France and the

---

*Sam Sary later joined the Khmer Serei traitor group.

strengthening of communism in Indochina is leading to dis-affection by Cambodian citizens. An increasing part of the population is crossing over to dissidents and the threat of a civil war similar to that raging in Vietnam is a real one."

The "dissidents" were of course members of the Nekhum Issarak Khmer (Khmer Freedom Front) which had been founded to carry on the anti-colonial struggle. After the French comeback in October 1945, the Front was immedi-ately supported in Phnom Penh by civil servants, workers and students—first in political actions, strikes and demonstra-tions, and in a more militant form later when an appeal was made for volunteers to leave the city and join the Khmer Issarak armed forces.

In August 1946, the latter struck their first real blow by wiping out the French garrison at Siem Reap and capturing the entire stock of arms. They gradually began to set up guerrilla bases, extending over large areas in northwest, southwest and southeast Cambodia (the same regions that the National United Front, formed after Sihanouk's overthrow in 1970, seized within a matter of weeks). At first their only arms were those captured from the enemy. Later they built jungle arsenals for the manufacture of small arms, hand grenades, mines, light bazookas and other weapons suitable for partisan warfare. Between 1946 and 1949, People's Committees were formed at district and village levels in many provinces, with self-defense units to protect the villages. As the organization developed, resistance groups in isolated areas were linked up; finally there was a large, united military-political front.*

In April 1950, an important political event took place. A Conference of People's Representatives was held, attended by 200 delegates from all sections of the population. Typical of the situation in Cambodia is the fact that over half (105, to

*These developments and many of the activities of the Khmer Issarak movement, I have described in detail in my book, *Mekong Upstream*, Fleuve Rouge Publishers, Hanoi, 1957; Seven Seas Books, Berlin, 1959.

be exact) were Buddhist bonzes.* The Conference decided to set up a Central Committee for Liberation, later transformed into a provisional government and subsequently into a Government of National Resistance, to administer the areas already under Khmer Issarak control.

On March 3, 1951 there was a conference of the Nekhum Issarak Khmer and parallel organizations in Vietnam and Laos. At this conference the Vietnam-Khmer-Lao Alliance was formed to coordinate the struggle in the three countries. It was on the basis of decisions taken at this conference that Vietnamese volunteers later entered Cambodia and Laos to fight the French side by side with the Khmer Issarak forces (by then the Khmer National Liberation Army) and the Pathet Lao, the Loation liberation forces. From that moment the resistance forces went from strength to strength. France's most illustrious soldier, General de Lattre de Tassigny was sent to Indochina where other lesser military stars had failed; he tried and also failed and was withdrawn after having lost virtually the whole of northern Laos. He was replaced in March 1953 by General Henri Navarre with the famous plan to "end the war in 18 months." Another 20,000 troops were sent from France for Navarre's "win the war" plan.

By this time there were 291 French battalions in Indochina. Of the 80 combat or mobile battalions, 71 were concentrated in Vietnam. Navarre withdrew all combat battalions from Cambodia but had to leave nine in Laos because of the intensified activities of the Pathet Lao and Vietminh. The strength of the static "pacification" forces remained at 30 battalions in Cambodia and Laos, with 181 stationed in Vietnam. But the forces in Cambodia were reduced to only two French battalions of "pacification troops" and five battalions of the Royal Khmer Army under French command.

---

*It is in the tradition of Cambodian Buddhism that the bonzes have played a consistently patriotic role. Thus it was a major setback for the Lon Nol-Sirik Matak regime that the Buddhist hierarchy and rank and file bonzes were immediately hostile to it and the hostility increased in proportion to the savagery of the repression.

Sihanouk (then King) used this situation, together with the mounting activities of the Khmer Issarak movement, to pressure the French for more and more concessions.

By this time (March 1953) the essential bone of contention between the French government of the day and Sihanouk was the question of Cambodia's adhesion to the French Union and the French demand to continue using Cambodia as a base for operations in Vietnam and Laos. To frighten Sihanouk, the French even created a false Issarak movement which committed terrorist acts aimed particularly at the Monarchy. The argument was then used that only the presence of French arms under a French command could save Cambodia and the Monarchy from destruction.

Sihanouk met this challenge head on, in a manner later to become characteristic. He secretly passed arms, and permitted some officers and men to desert, to the real Khmer Issarak forces. In a note to the French President on March 5, 1953 Sihanouk showed that he was aware of French policy to reconquer the former Indochinese colonies one at a time. In it he stressed the strength of the Khmer Issarak movement, the popular basis of its support and his refusal to permit Cambodia to become involved in France's fight with the Vietminh.

"The present policy of France in Indochina," he wrote, "is based on the idea that the principal aim at the moment is success in the fight against the Vietminh." He pointed out that such a policy was not for Cambodia where the people "above all desire peace and are sincerely attached to the ideas of liberty and independence. The real situation from a military and political viewpoint," he continued, "is the following: Three-fifths of our territory are occupied by the Vietminh," the term Sihanouk used loosely to describe the Cambodian and Vietnamese resistance forces. The only solution, he pointed out, was complete independence to deprive the Vietminh and Khmer Issarak of their popular support. He stressed that the Khmer Issarak had deep roots among the people:

"Native sons, peasants and even townspeople . . . their patriotic proclamations find a favorable response among the

people and also among the [Buddhist] clergy whose influence is enormous throughout the kingdom. They are
assured of faithful followers among the masses as well as
amongst the nation's elite. . . . The Issarak danger is real in
itself. These rebels frequently mount ambushes against our
patrols of provincial guards, police and troops and recently—
alone or together with the Vietminh—have obtained results
which have greatly affected public opinion by the assassination of a governor, a chief of province and district chiefs."
(Among those killed was the French High Commissioner for
Cambodia, de Raymond, assassinated in Phnom Penh by a
Khmer Issarak guerrilla in November 1951.)

Sihanouk referred to the fake French-created Issarak,
which included a member of the royal family "and who even
receive supplies and arms from the French Command, while
the leader of this band (a Prince Chantarainsey) is in constant
contact with senior French officers with whom he dines on
occasion."

The main grounds on which the Khmer Issarak found such
wide support among the population, Sihanouk points out in
his note, was that Cambodia was not really independent.
"What can I reply," he asks, "when the Issarak propaganda
proves to the people and the clergy that Cambodia is not
really independent?" He made very detailed suggestions for
the "transfer of prerogatives till now withheld by France and
which in consequence would make it incumbent on the King
and the Royal Government to find themselves the means
necessary to exercize their powers and responsibilities." Only
by such a step, he said, could French policy "be understood
and accepted by our people who, I must stress, have
developed considerably and demand more than ever the real
attributes of independence." Attached to the note were two
appendices, one outlining Sihanouk's ideas for more independence in military, judicial, financial and economic affairs,
the other regarding the "tacit agreement" between the
French High Command and the spurious Issarak movement.*

---

*This movement was the forerunner to the Khmer Serei, run by the
CIA. At that time, the false Issarak also had close ties with the Black
Dragon Society, a sort of Japanese super-CIA.

At this time Sihanouk was just 30, but already displaying considerable talent for statesmanship which must have appalled French policy-makers. In 1941, when Sihanouk's grandfather, Sisowath Monivong, died it was the French as king-makers who selected the 19-years-old Norodom Sihanouk to succeed him instead of his uncle, the older and tougher Prince Sisowath Monireth.* At one of the informal receptions that Sihanouk delighted in arranging for diplomats and journalists, he once commented regarding his accession to the throne, "The French chose me because they thought I was a little lamb. Later they were surprised to discover that I was a tiger. In fact I was always a tiger—but at that time a little one."

When he got no reply to the March 5 note and there was no reaction to the complaint about Prince Chantarainsey's band of fake Issarak, Sihanouk sent a second note on March 18, 1953 which he described as a "cry of alarm," citing the "desertion" to the Khmer Issarak of a lieutenant of the Royal Army with 40 soldiers and their equipment. He cautioned that if France did not immediately revise its policy the whole of Cambodia would rally to the "rebels." The "desertion" was Sihanouk's way of hitting back at the French High Command for forming the spurious Issarak forces. It was a clear warning also that if independence were not granted immediately, the whole of the Royal Army might go over to the real Khmer Issarak to get independence by force of arms.

The French reply came within 24 hours, an invitation from President Auriol for Sihanouk to lunch with him at Versailles on March 25. At the luncheon Sihanouk's demands for speedy negotiations to give substance to Cambodia's independence were rejected and he was told bluntly to clear out of France and go home as quickly as possible. The communique issued by the President, while full of the usual platitudes about the great friendship which animated the discussions, ended with a curious admonition that Sihanouk "should return to Phnom

*It is ironic that 29 years later, the Americans, fancying themselves as the new king-makers, chose Prince Sisowath Sirik Matak, nephew of Monireth, as their "strong man" in Phnom Penh.

Penh within a few days." This was the last thing that
Sihanouk intended. The minimum he wanted was agreement
in principle on a new basis for Cambodian-French relations.
The Minister for Associated States also told Sihanouk to go
home, his continued presence in France was not desired and
would be interpreted as "pressure on the French Government." Sihanouk did not go home, but went to the United
States where his demands for support for Cambodian
independence were received coldly and unsympathetically by
John Foster Dulles. The latter also told him in effect to go
home and help General Navarre win the war against the
"communists."*

In an interview with the *New York Times* after he arrived
in Washington, Sihanouk repeated that only full independence would satisfy the Cambodian people. Replying to
questions as to whether he was not aware of the communist
menace, he said: "Among intellectual circles of the Cambodian people there has been created a growing conviction
that the Vietminh Communists fight for the independence of
their country." He added that such elements "did not want
to die for the French and help them to remain in Cambodia."
Again, he made a passionate plea for total independence.

This revealed a line which Sihanouk has followed consistently until today. A man's attitude toward his country and
people was the important thing, not his ideology. National
interests come before class interests. He recognized that the
Vietminh then as the Vietcong today were patriots, fighting
for the true independence of their country. He refused to
make any concessions, even in return for Cambodia's
independence, which would help France then (or the United
States today) to crush that armed struggle.

Sihanouk returned from the United States disgusted and
disillusioned, not only by the official derision with which his
requests for support were received, but also by evidence of
racial discrimination which he personally experienced. The

---

*Details of this whole revealing episode in Sihanouk's diplomatic
struggle for real independence were given the author on Sihanouk's
personal instructions for the book, *Mekong Upstream*.

New York Times interview caused much "pain" in Paris, but as it coincided with severe military reverses in Vietnam the French Government made a show of starting talks on the points raised by Sihanouk. It was soon clear that no serious negotiations were really intended and the talks were quickly bogged down by interminable delays in referring every question to Paris. On June 14, 1953 Sihanouk left Phnom Penh abruptly for Bangkok to alert world opinion and, as he expressed it, "to give a final warning to the French." In a note distributed to foreign embassies in Bangkok (obviously, there were none at that time in Phnom Penh) Sihanouk made the point that the people as a whole from the peasants to the intellectual elite, including the army and Buddhist clergy, were all for complete independence "even if this means a general revolt to throw off the yoke of the French occupiers."

In a forceful expression of patriotism and providing a rare example of a monarch engaged in self-criticism, King Sihanouk admitted that he had been wrong to sign a convention in 1949 which included clauses limiting Cambodian sovereignty and placed the country within the French Union. "I am grateful," he stated, "that the people have not punished me for acting against their will in placing our country in the French Union and for having violated the sovereignty of our country by accepting the treaty of 1949. In this decisive turning point in the history of our country and our relations with France, I must choose between France and my compatriots. Obviously, I choose my compatriots."

Based on several long discussions with the Cambodian leader in the first years after independence, I made the following assessment in *Mekong Upstream*, written in 1956, at a time when there was considerable suspicion in progressive circles and in the socialist camp about Sihanouk and the genuineness of his neutrality.

"He is a vigorous and intelligent personality who thinks for himself and says what he thinks with frankness and courage. He shows considerable ability in adapting himself to changing situations and tends to view problems with an open mind and to learn as he goes along. He shows an independence of judgement which has appalled certain diplomats at the moment when they were certain they had gained their point. He is not afraid to admit mistakes nor to take quick measures to correct them. His enemies say he is self-willed and will not tolerate opposition; those who know him best say his character has mellowed considerably since he traveled abroad and gained experience in statesmanship. No one questions that Sihanouk is a true patriot and that his self-will and obstinacy are largely expressed by his uncompromising stand for full independence and nothing less.

"I have had the pleasure of several conversations with Sihanouk and the outstanding impressions are his frankness, his ability to express himself with clarity and eloquence and his grasp of an idea or trend of thought before one has half finished expressing it. He speaks excellent French and English and is not averse to using apt quotes from the French classics to illustrate a point."

After knowing him considerably better during the 14 years that have elapsed since, I have little to add as to the main traits of his character.

Paralleling the diplomatic struggle carried on by Sihanouk in this period was the struggle waged on the military-political front by the Khmer Issarak and their Vietminh allies. Among the most effective recruits for the Khmer Issarak armed forces were the rubber plantation workers. Of a total labor force of about 12,000 on the plantations—herded behind barbed wire and escorted to work by armed guards—some 1,500 had escaped to join the resistance. In the forests neighboring the plantations, in the Chup area near the Vietnamese frontier, the Khmer Issarak had set up arsenals for making grenades and other arms, staffed almost entirely by the plantation workers. Guerrilla units were formed from former plantation workers in villages surrounding the region and regular liaison was maintained with a Khmer Issarak headquarters established inside the biggest of the three Chup plantations, under the very eyes of the French.

It is therefore not surprising that after Sihanouk was overthrown in 1970, the plantation workers from the same region were among the first to set up armed units and that large areas were liberated within a few days. In view of the contention by the Americans and the Lon Nol-Sirik Matak regime that the trouble in Cambodia is due to "aggression" from North Vietnam, it is worth repeating the account given by a veteran Khmer Issarak cadre and which I published at the time in *Mekong Upstream*. Summing up the role of the rubber plantation workers at the time of the resistance struggle against the French, he said:

"They represent the largest single mass of proletariat that we have in Cambodia. You know that we have no real industry and so no industrial workers. At first some of us tended to overlook this potential because the regular plantation workers are mostly Vietnamese. Cambodians work there mainly between the agricultural seasons to supplement their incomes. Some of us thought it would be difficult to create a single effective organization. The French had long tried to divide Cambodians and Vietnamese by offering big rewards if the Cambodians would denounce Vietnamese fleeing from the plantations. Their propaganda was that the Vietminh wanted to conquer Cambodia. . . . In the beginning there were difficulties. It took a lot of patient and dangerous work to establish the first contacts and explain the situation. But the results were magnificent and above all complete solidarity between Cambodian and Vietnamese workers was achieved. The French propaganda failed because the Cambodians saw in day-to-day activities the self-sacrificing way in which Vietnamese workers defended the common interests. They fought shoulder to shoulder against the real enemy.

"During the last years of the war, plantation workers provided two-thirds of the staff for all of our secret production bases, for almost all our transport corps, for liaison work not only throughout all east Cambodia but also with the fronts in South Vietnam."[*]

---

[*]The Cambodian working class has developed considerably since those days and so has the solidarity between Cambodian and Vietnamese workers, not only on the plantations. It was no coincidence that the first large-scale massacre of Cambodians by Lon Nol's troops in March 1970 was in Kompong Cham province, where the rubber plantations are situated.

What with the deteriorating military situation in Vietnam and the increasing activities of the Khmer Issarak inside Cambodia the Laniel-Bidault government in Paris started negotiations again. Some progress was made toward giving Cambodia independence but there were provisos that would have given the French High Command the right to use Cambodia as an operational base against the Vietminh. The formula was the reservation of "temporary facilities for the necessary means of assuring operational command of units stationed east of the Mekong."

"East of the Mekong" covered the whole of Vietnam, almost all of Laos and about a third of Cambodia. Sihanouk fought tooth and nail against such conditions and bluntly refused to accept independence until they were dropped. As the French High Command was anxious for a settlement with Cambodia so that troops there could be transferred to other fronts, the provisos eventually were dropped. While negotiations were still proceeding Sihanouk's senior adviser and then prime minister, Penn Nouth, made an appeal in the King's name which resulted for the first time in the label of "neutralist" being pinned on the Cambodian leader. The appeal was made on July 31, 1953 for fighting to cease on Cambodian soil:

"Although we are not communists, we do not oppose communism as long as the latter is not to be imposed on our people by force from outside. ... What happens in Vietnam is none of our business." In other words, Sihanouk made clear that even at the price of an indefinite postponement of independence, he had no intention of taking part in an anti-communist or anti-Vietminh crusade or of permitting Cambodian territory to be used in such a crusade.

Le Monde commented with. prophetic insight: "Washington does not hide the fact that its whole policy in Southeast Asia is in danger from a wave of neutralism which the example of Cambodia has just launched." Washington has still not overcome that fear of the spread of neutralism in Southeast Asia, denounced by the late John Foster Dulles as "immoral and dangerous."

Another quality of Sihanouk's with which Washington will

have to grapple now that Cambodian neutrality has been swept aside, is one that I also noted in *Mekong Upstream*, the first book I wrote about Cambodian problems.

"There are abundant signs that Sihanouk realizes that while nothing can be done without the people, everything can be done with them. In every crisis Sihanouk has appealed to the people and the people have responded. Each time Sihanouk moves closer to the people, the people move closer to Sihanouk."

American intervention in Cambodian affairs started immediately after the horrifying discovery of Sihanouk's neutralism in mid-1953. The ultra-reactionary head of the China Lobby, Senator Knowland, and U.S. Ambassador to Saigon, Donald Heath, were dispatched to reason with Prime Minister Penn Nouth and convince him of the necessity of joining in the anti-communist crusade. Penn Nouth repeated Sihanouk's views that Cambodia "had nothing against communist regimes as long as they do not interfere with Cambodia." Knowland's arguments that this was a dangerous policy, that one should not await the danger but go out to meet it by attacking "communists and Vietminh" made no impression. Heath added that the urgency of the fight against communism demanded that Cambodia agree to France having the sole military command for Cambodia, as well as Laos and Vietnam. Penn Nouth, with Sihanouk's backing, refused. The Knowland-Heath visit marked the beginning of prolonged and intensive U.S. interference in Cambodia's internal affairs, soon to take the form of attempts to do away with Sihanouk and his brand of neutrality.

By November 1953 Sihanouk had warned that Cambodia would withdraw from the French Union unless all powers, including full military authority and responsibility for internal and external security, were transferred to Cambodia. On November 9 agreement was reached on essential powers being transferred, the French retaining some temporary transit rights for their troops but they were forced to abandon the demand for bases for their operational commands "east of the Mekong."

On November 20, General Navarre started dropping

parachute troops under Colonel Christian de Castries into the valley of Dien Bien Phu, as the key move in a vast operation aimed at reoccupying northern Laos and all of northern Vietnam, and thus win the war. The Dien Bien Phu operation, intended as the decisive element of the "Navarre Plan," ended in the historic victory for the Vietnamese People's Army on May 7, 1954, the very day ceasefire discussions opened at Geneva—an example of Ho Chi Minh's military-political planning, rare in the annals of history.

At the Geneva Conference, France's ill-fated Foreign Minister Georges Bidault blandly tried to prove that there was no such thing as a war in Indochina. France had been engaged merely in putting down "communist subversion" there and in helping the "independent" states of Cambodia and Laos defend themselves against "Vietminh agression"! Not very different really from Washington's official apologia for waging war against the peoples of Indochina 16 years later.

The foreign minister of the Democratic Republic of Vietnam, Pham Van Dong, showed that his government had no designs against Cambodia and Laos by offering to withdraw all Vietminh forces immediately upon the conclusion of a ceasefire, providing the governments of Cambodia and Laos agreed to ban the establishment of foreign military bases on their soil. It was not difficult for Pham Van Dong to justify this demand since the French and Japanese had consistently used one of the three states as a base for the invasion of the others. This was agreed. At Geneva, recognition of the real independence and sovereignty of Vietnam, Cambodia and Laos was written into international documents for the first time.

The Geneva Conference marked the end of an entire historic phase for Cambodia, and for Indochina as a whole. A new phase was to be ushered in with the United States taking over the self-appointed task of "filling the power vacuum" caused by the French collapse.

3
Background to the March Coup

Apart from Sihanouk's own experiences in the United States and the Knowland-Heath pressures recounted in the previous chapter, the first collision with Washington came soon after the 1954 Geneva Agreements put an end to the first war in Indochina.

Cambodia at the end of the war needed economic and financial assistance. The government, which had never been able to get its fingers on the country's assets, was left with a bankrupt economy and empty coffers. There was no money to pay the army or administration. Washington offered dollar aid which Sihanouk agreed to accept as long as it was without conditions. He was insistent on this point. The American negotiators probably winked at each other and said, "We'll give the aid now and send in the bill later." The bill proved to be Cambodia's membership of SEATO.* Sihanouk refused to pay it and thereupon his real difficulties with the United States began.

There are differences of opinion among Cambodian progressives about the extent to which aid was needed and the way in which it should have been spent. The main expense was the army. Until independence, military expenses were paid in theory by the French but from funds poured into France by Washington to keep the war going. With the end of

*Southeast Asia Treaty Organization; set up in Manila in September 1954 by the United States, Britain, France, Australia, New Zealand, the Philippines, Thailand and Pakistan.

the war, the payments were made directly to Cambodia from Washington. American pressures were first exerted in the form of warnings that the "Vietminh" or Chinese "Reds" were about to attack Cambodia—making imperative the expansion of the army, especially as French troops were no longer around. The U.S. government would be only too happy to foot the bill. So the army was expanded and modernized and fitted out mainly with American equipment.

Communications were in a bad state. Cambodia's only outlet to the sea was along the Mekong River through South Vietnam. Although she had 250 miles of coastline along the Gulf of Siam, there were no deep-water ports, nor roads or railways linking the coast with the interior (apart from the line which led from Phnom Penh, 100 miles south to the seaside resort of Kep). The Americans financed railway construction in both Thailand and Cambodia to provide a rail link between Phnom Penh and Bangkok. But Cambodia, with historically bad experiences at the hands of her two neighbors, did not wish to be dependent on South Vietnam and Thailand for her communications with the outside world. She wanted her own port. The idea suited the French also, as American pressures started to squeeze French interests out of Saigon and threatened French trade with Cambodia via the Mekong.

France agreed with Sihanouk's request to build a port at the tiny fishing village of Kompong Som on the Gulf of Siam, where the water was deep enough for ocean-going vessels. Sihanouk wanted to use some of the U.S. aid to build a railroad from the future port to the interior. American aid experts vetoed the proposal on the ground that "strategically" it would be dangerous to have a railroad leading in from the sea. "Red" China might invade that way! However, the Americans were not averse to building railroads from Thailand or improving communications with South Vietnam, whence had come the only invasions in the past. After much discussion the Americans agreed to construct a road if the French built the port. Port and road were the main features of the economic side of the foreign aid program. That

Sihanouk should have fought so hard for this is consistent with his single-minded determination to fight for the country's real independence, a goal he never abandoned.

Dollars were also provided to finance imports. Cambodian importers paid into a special counterfund the equivalent in local currency for the dollars they drew to pay for imports. The counterfund was controlled entirely by U.S. aid officials, to be used as they liked: "The greatest invention since the wheel," was how one aid enthusiast once described it. The counterfund was used to pay the Cambodian army and for U.S. aid projects such as the road; the salaries, rents, etc. of the Americans who began to swarm into Phnom Penh, and also—as was discovered later—to finance extensive CIA activities inside the country. The first U.S. ambassador to Cambodia after 1954, Robert McClintock, was a top CIA agent as was also his chief aide at the Phnom Penh embassy, Martin F. Herz. These two, in effect, controlled the counterfund budget.

On March 3, 1955 Sihanouk abdicated as King, in favor of his father, Norodom Suramarit. He did so in a typical surprise move by sending an envelope to the Phnom Penh radio station, asking the program director to play the tape enclosed in place of the customary midday newscast. He had recorded his speech of abdication. Even to those closest to him, this came as a complete surprise. I saw him shortly afterward and asked why he had taken this step. His reply revealed much of his inner thinking and explains many of his statements after the March 18 coup.

"I wanted to offer proof to our young people, especially our young students," he said, "that my efforts for the country and nation had nothing to do with the wish to be his Majesty the King, or to my attachment to the throne."

There is no question that, in fact, he chose this manner to end the monarchy in a dignified, if protracted way, and to play a more direct role in the country's affairs. He believed this was the only way to ensure the country's independence after the war in view of American attempts, which became quickly apparent, to replace France in Indochina. As his father had no other heirs, and Sihanouk gave a pledge that he would not accept the throne again after his father's death, the Monarchy as an institution would end with the death of Sihanouk's parents. To all practical purposes, except for important traditions which have value as a unifying factor, the Monarchy ended with Sihanouk's abdication. (At the May 5, 1970 press conference at which Sihanouk announced the formation of a Royal Government of National Union, he said: "In form we are a monarchy, but the content is republican.")

In the same abdication broadcast, Sihanouk annouced the formation of the Sangkum (Popular Socialist Community) formed by the fusion of existing political parties into what was to become virtually the only legal political movement in the country. Through the Sangkum, Sihanouk reaffirmed that Cambodian foreign policy would be based on strict neutrality.

Broadcasting to the nation two weeks after his abdication, Sihanouk also revealed his patriotism, his realism and his desire and capacity to adjust himself to new situations.

"When I assigned myself the task to struggle against foreign domination," he said, "confronted as I was with the great powers, my royal authority was necessary to facilitate my task and to wage a successful struggle for the fatherland. ... If I had not spoken as King of Cambodia, they could always have replied that I did not represent Cambodia, but only a clique or a part of national opinion." He explained that the situation had since changed and the main problems to be solved were those concerning Cambodia's internal developments.

"If I remained on the throne," he continued, "locked up in my palace, no matter how great my affection for the people or my desire to help them, I would never really know their true situation or the abuses of which they may be victims. I would be unable to distinguish the true from the false, black from white, justice from injustice, truth from slander. A sovereign has far too high a position for the people to be able to see him often. Even if the people succeeded in being received by the King, they would not expose the real source of their griefs because they are always accompanied by officials and so they fear reprisals. How can the monarch know what happens to the people after they leave the palace?

"Also the palace is stuffed full of a whole hierarchy of court mandarins, amongst whom slide the intriguers, like blood-sucking leeches that fasten themselves to the feet of elephants. Such conditions make it quite impossible for the monarch to render justice to the people. For one thing, the latter dare not open their hearts; for another, certain highly placed persons are always on hand awaiting the propitious moment to give the King advice which is not necessarily in the interests of the people."

In this very detailed explanation as to the reasons for his abdication, Sihanouk explained that he had tried to have contact with the people; that he was deeply interested in their problems but "by the very fact that I was King, every time I wanted to travel I had to notify the administrative authorities so they could take what they considered necessary measures in advance. They organized official convoys, they mobilized troops and police, they cleaned up the khets and khands (provinces and districts) according to the exact itinerary of my visit. ... After a speech, it is practically impossible for the sovereign to contact the people and get any information because the officials are sure to have taken the necessary precautions to make everything seem right and proper."

This was not demagogy on Sihanouk's part. He has always sought the closest contact with the people. After he had rid himself of the trappings of a monarch, he delighted to drop in—quite literally by a tiny helicopter—unannounced on places he considered of interest at the moment. He visited every corner of the country, literally every district, many of them repeatedly, and had that intimate contact with the people right up to the moment of his overthrow, of a quality that very few leaders could claim. When I visited him in Peking, shortly after the March 18 coup, Sihanouk said that it was the contact with the people that he missed most, in his temporary exile. He recalled that he was in the habit of spending two to three days every week in the provinces.

It is the spirit of the 1955 abdication speech that his announcement from Peking, 15 years later, that he would not seek office as Chief of State again, must be seen. He realized that a whole era had come to an end and a new one was starting in which neither the type of regime he had headed in the past, nor that which had usurped its powers, would have a place. The future belonged to the people, but first there must be a struggle for real national liberation, in which Sihanouk pledged to take part on the side of the people. There is no doubt that he has long been an admirer of Prince Souphanouvong in Laos for having led such a long and arduous resistance struggle with all the hardships and sacrifices that this entailed.

By the end of 1955, pressure on Cambodia to join SEATO began to reach outrageous proportions. There was direct pressure on Sihanouk himself from John Foster Dulles and when this did not work, brother Allen, then head of the CIA, came to Phnom Penh with "proofs" of impending "communist aggression," the only protection against which would be membership in SEATO. Sihanouk replied that the 1954 Geneva Agreements provided for Cambodian neutrality. Dulles knew very well that without Cambodian agreement and U.S. military power solidly implanted in that country up to the borders of South Vietnam, SEATO would be ineffective as an instrument of domination of the area. Cambodia represented a "missing link" in the chain of anti-communist "bastions" Dulles was forging across South Asia from the Philippines to Thailand.

I arrived in Phnom Penh in March 1956 when pressures were building up to their climax. Sihanouk had outraged the State Department when he paid an official visit to Peking, despite an arrogant warning by Ambassador McClintock. Work on the famous road from Sihanoukville, already taking shape as a port, had still not started and Washington was threatening to cut off economic aid altogether. To stress how dependent Cambodia was on the goodwill of the United

States and its allies, South Vietnam and Thailand had closed their frontiers with Cambodia and started an economic blockade. U.S. planes, officially taking part in SEATO maneuvers in Thailand, daily were violating Cambodian air space. Khmer Serei irregulars, another of the CIA's private armies, were making raids into Cambodia from bases in Thailand and infiltrating agents and saboteurs from South Vietnam. The newly-arrived U.S. ambassador to Bangkok was the same Peurifoy who had engineered the overthrow of the independent-minded government of Guatemala in 1954 (after it had expropriated 234,000 acres of land held by the United Fruit Company).

I wrote a series of articles describing the situation in Cambodia as ominously reminiscent to that on the eve of the CIA-sponsored action in Guatemala. Some articles were picked up and extracts were rebroadcast over Peking and Hanoi radios. John Foster Dulles took it upon himself to deny one of these in a letter to the Cambodian foreign ministry on April 15, 1956 in which he expressed "alarm that statements from various sources are giving increasing publicity to allegations according to which the United States tried to force Cambodia into joining the SEATO pact by threatening to withdraw U.S. economic aid and that the United States had obliged independent and friendly nations such as Vietnam and Thailand to impose measures of economic warfare against Cambodia." Dulles denounced such allegations as "completely false" and warned that they "could damage the friendly relations existing between our two states." He pointed out that the U.S. ambassador to Cambodia had brought to the knowledge of the King and Queen some days earlier that "the United States has never publicly made any official observations concerning Cambodian neutrality."

That was one of the moments when a journalist has a sinking feeling in his stomach, starts checking again the facts on which his articles were based and reassesses the reliability of his sources. How many Heads of State will stand up against a demarché from a U.S. Secretary of State? But

Sihanouk immediately published a declaration, in the first point of which he observed that it was curious for Dulles to reply to newspaper articles by a letter to the Cambodian foreign ministry. He then dealt with the matter of "no public or official" U.S. observations on Cambodian neutrality.

"It is difficult to be more prudent," Sihanouk commented. "It is a fact that 'officially' and 'publicly' the United States has never made any observations about Cambodian neutrality. However private American 'advice' and unofficial 'criticism' have not been lacking. ... It so happens that I have in my hands overwhelming proof of a plot in Manila against Cambodian neutrality."

He went on to reveal an extraordinary incident during his official visit to the Philippines a few months earlier when "an unknown person not of Philippines nationality" had presented Sihanouk with an amended version of his own speech, rewritten on U.S. Embassy notepaper, and which he was scheduled to deliver the following day at the Camp Murphy headquarters of the Philippine Army. The amended version of the speech was full of phrases about the necessity for "cooperating with other free countries against communist aggression or subversion," and the like. The Manila press had been running banner headlines to the effect that Sihanouk had come to the Philippines to announce Cambodia's entry into SEATO. This was the limit. Sihanouk refused the draft, reverting to his own original text, the essence of which was that Cambodia "cannot take part in any military blocs because of the agreements freely signed at Geneva" and that Cambodia "despite ideological differences, would maintain correct relations with all other powers on the basis of non-interference in each other's affairs, the only solid basis for lasting peace." He was warned that to make such a speech "would offend his hosts." But he insisted. He was prevented from delivering the speech; the ceremony at Camp Murphy was cancelled, and he was subject to humiliating insults for the rest of his stay for refusing to please his hosts—and the American backers of his hosts—by announcing Cambodia's entry into SEATO.

All this was spelt out in great length and detail for the benefit of the late John Foster Dulles and, as a sort of footnote to the whole affair, Sihanouk gave me an exclusive interview in which he categorically rejected SEATO "protection" of Cambodia or any relationship whatsoever with SEATO. It was the most definite and all-embracing rejection of SEATO he had ever made. He coupled that statement with another, in the same interview, to the effect that he would welcome entering into diplomatic relations with the Soviet Union and other countries of the socialist world. (At that time only SEATO powers were represented in Phnom Penh, with the exception of India, very strongly neutral at that time.) American-inspired pressures were stepped up again from this time on and took more specific forms.

In 1956, the site of a famous Angkorian-period temple at Preah Vihear on Cambodia's northern frontier with Thailand was seized by Thailand and Sihanouk was only restrained by American pressures from sending his army to expel the Thai occupying forces. Two years later, South Vietnamese troops of Ngo Dinh Diem invaded Cambodia's northernmost province of Stung Treng, penetrating to a depth of 10 miles and showing every intention of staying. Sihanouk ordered his troops into action to repel them, but was informed by the head of the U.S. military aid mission that American arms, even in Cambodian hands, could not be used against America's allies, Thailand or South Vietnam. Nor could American military trucks be used to transport Cambodian troops for such operations.

Sihanouk discovered to his horror that not only could arms and transport supplied under the U.S. military aid program not be used to defend Cambodia against the only imaginable sources of danger to the country but that this "aid" would be cut off completely if Cambodia accepted any military aid from other countries. He defied the Americans on this occasion, exerting enough military pressure to force the invaders out.

The following year a major CIA plot to overthrow Sihanouk was discovered and put down due to good intelligence work backed by warnings from Chinese and French intelligence services and to the loyalty of the people's militia in Siem Reap province, where the Angkor ruins are located. The plotters included a Cambodian Colonel Dap Chhuon; Ngo Dinh Diem's brother-in-law who was South Vietnam's consul in Phnom Penh; the head of the Khmer Serei traitor group, Son Ngoc Thanh (an old agent of the Japanese and U.S. intelligence services)* and his close associate, Sam Sary, former Cambodian ambassador in London. (The latter had been recalled following a scandal arising from his severe beating of a Cambodian serving girl at the Embassy whom he had made pregnant.) The plot was master-minded by an American CIA agent at the U.S. Embassy in Phnom Penh, Victor Masao Matsui.

The rebel headquarters was raided in time. Large stocks of arms, a quantity of small gold ingots for buying collaborators, and incriminating documents were found. Dap Chhuon was wounded by one of his own men in the surprise attack and, according to accounts later, he asked for a high-ranking officer to whom he wanted to make a statement on the background of the plot which would have incriminated Lon Nol. The latter, then head of the Cambodian army, sent someone to finish off Dap Chhuon with a bullet in the head. Matsui was expelled for espionage (seven years later he was expelled from Karachi for the same reason). The

---

*Son Ngoc Thanh had been puppet prime minister of Cambodia under the Japanese. Later he tried to capture the leadership of the Khmer Issarak movement. When that failed he joined the false Khmer Issarak set up by the French. Later he fled to Thailand and from then on offered his services to the United States. He founded and headed the Khmer Serei (Free Cambodia) traitor group subsidized and armed by the CIA. First based in Saigon he later transferred to Thailand from where he directed armed sabotage against Cambodia. After the March 18 coup, he returned to Phnom Penh with units of the Khmer Serei armed forces as the backbone of Lon Nol's shock troops. It was rumored that part of the "price" demanded by the Saigon regime for military support for Phnom Penh was that Son Ngoc Thanh should replace Lon Nol as prime minister.

essence of the plot was to seize, as a start, the northernmost provinces of Cambodia, declare an alliance with the southern provinces of Laos—then under a faithful U.S. ally, Prince Boun Oum of Champassac—and declare an independent secessionist state to be recognized immediately by the United States. At that time a group of U.S. policy-planners were working on the idea of a "corridor" through southern Laos to link South Vietnam with Thailand, as a second-best alternative to bringing Cambodia into SEATO.*

Later in the same year, a "present" in the form of a charming lacquered box arrived for the Queen Mother, marked to be opened by her personally. Whoever sent it knew her habit of opening her own mail, usually in the presence of her husband and Sihanouk. On this occasion, because Prime Minister Son Sann had arrived unexpectedly to bid farewell before a trip abroad, the mail was opened in an anteroom. A few seconds before Sihanouk arrived to join his parents in the throne room, there was a tremendous explosion; the King's secretary was blown to bits as he opened the lacquered box-bomb, and another attendant was killed underneath the throne room by the force of the explosion. From what was left of the wrappings, it was learned that the bomb had been mailed from a U.S. military post office in Saigon.

Sihanouk was beginning to learn the quality of U.S. "aid." As a first step he closed down the U.S. military mission. This took place after another incident in which a number of wooden cases addressed to the U.S. Embassy, normally not inspected because of diplomatic immunity, were found to be

*According to one version, which I heard in Cambodia at the time, Lon Nol was involved; once the secessionist state was consolidated and recognized, he intended to carry out a coup and attach the rest of Cambodia to the secessionist state. Sihanouk seems not to accept this version. At his May 6, 1970 Peking press conference he referred to the Dap Chhuon plot to "wage a war of secession" but said that Lon Nol had helped him "to crush this rebellion." That an officer of Lon Nol's staff inexplicably silenced the wounded Dap Chhuon is well known in Cambodian army circles.

full of arms. They were destined for Khmer Serei groups being infiltrated into Cambodia from South Vietnam at that time.

In 1963 Sihanouk obtained unanimous approval from the National Assembly to renounce all U.S. economic and military aid. It had become all too clear that this was being used to strangle the country's economic development, especially as it could not be used to finance the state enterprises which the government of those days favored. Instead, it was being used to develop a class of compradore capitalists with a vested interest in U.S. aid at any price and thus actively or potentially hostile to Sihanouk's nationalist policies. It was known by this time that the counterpart funds were being employed to finance CIA operations throughout the country in which many of the 300 American members of the various "aid" missions were involved.

The following year there was a major scandal when the manager of the Phnom Penh bank, Song Sak, later identified as the top CIA agent inside the country, was discovered to be up to his neck in economic and financial sabotage. Avoiding arrest, he escaped to Saigon where he immediately joined Son Ngoc Thanh and Sam Sary as Number 3 man in the Khmer Serei leadership. Song Sak was closely associated with Sirik Matak and Yem Sambour, both of whom were known for their pro-American leanings and who became first and second deputy-premiers respectively in the Lon Nol cabinet after the March 18 coup.

Throughout this period, the United States had refused to recognize Cambodian neutrality or the country's territorial integrity within its present frontiers. Washington implicitly supported the Saigon regime's territorial claims against Cambodia, including claims on some small islands a few miles off the coast at the Kep seaside resort.

In February 1965 the Americans started the systematic bombing of North Vietnam, and a month later the first U.S. Marine detachments disembarked at Danang in South Vietnam. Direct U.S. intervention in South Vietnam and the air war against the North had started. Air and artillery strikes against Cambodian border villages were stepped up. Sihanouk threatened several times to sever diplomatic relations unless they were halted. They continued, and in May 1965, following the sacking of the U.S. Embassy in Phnom Penh, Sihanouk broke off diplomatic relations with the United States.

A U.S. plane, a helicopter and a tank, symbols of those shot down or destroyed on Cambodian territory, were put on public display in Phnom Penh as a reminder of what Cambodia had suffered from the United States only because she insisted on preserving her independence and neutrality and on living in peace within her own well-defined frontiers.

With the closing of the doors of the U.S. Embassy, an entire phase of Khmer-American relations ended—a bitterly disillusioning phase as far as Cambodia was concerned. The only ones in Phnom Penh who really regretted the American departure were those in American pay and the profiteers and speculators who had invested ill-gotten fortunes in building houses to let at high rents to American diplomats and staff members of the various U.S. missions.

4

Explanations

At an historic press conference in Peking on May 5, 1970 Prince Sihanouk announced the formation of a Government of National Union to lead a resistance struggle against those who had seized power in Phnom Penh on March 18 and against the forces they had called in to maintain them in power. He also reviewed some of the events which, in his view, had led to his overthrow. Describing the situation prior to the coup, he said: "Even if we were poor, our Cambodian people lived in peace and independence and in harmonious relations with other foreign residents." He then went on to contrast this with the racist, genocidal policies of the new Phnom Penh regime; the horrors of war that had been brought to Cambodia, and the fact that within six weeks, the country had been transformed into a U.S. colony—even into a sub-colony of South Vietnam. Referring to the leaders of the new regime, General Lon Nol and Prince Sirik Matak, Sihanouk said:

"You may well ask, from where do they come? Were they not your closest collaborators? Yes, it is true they were. Lon Nol was my right arm. We followed the same road from the time of our youth, from the time of the French Protectorate. With our esteemed elder brother, Penn Nouth [seated alongside Sihanouk at the press conference as Prime Minister of the newly formed resistance government], Lon Nol and I worked for our country's independence. We succeeded in forcing France to transfer her remaining colonial prerogatives to us in November 1953, eight months before the Geneva Conference on Indochina. It was Penn Nouth who signed the agreement on the transfer of France's remaining powers and

48

the complete withdrawal of French forces from Cambodia.

"Of course, it was not only Penn Nouth, Lon Nol and Sihanouk. We were three patriots among many others who fought and worked for the same aims. Our Cambodian people made great sacrifices and worked very hard. We also render homage to the heroic struggle of the Vietnamese people, under the leadership of President Ho Chi Minh, who greatly weakened French colonialism and thus facilitated the success of my own activities in obtaining full independence for our country. Our Cambodian people have always loved and admired my elder brother, Penn Nouth, because he is a true patriot, an upright, honorable man who has never wavered on the question of independence and devotion to the people. That is why the elected representatives of the people, our members of parliament, have always voted for Penn Nouth as Prime Minister.

"As for Lon Nol, I had entrusted him with the post of Commander-in-Chief of our armed forces. Premier Penn Nouth also had confidence in him. As Minister of National Defense, Lon Nol was responsible for national security. He was responsible for the armed forces and the state police. Lon Nol's recent plot, however, was not the first organized by the CIA against me. There was a whole series of plots because I was a neutralist who refused to give way to the Americans and who thus represented a danger to U.S. imperialism in Southeast Asia. . . . With Lon Nol faithful to me, the army faithful to Lon Nol and the people behind us, we were able to thwart all their plots. . . . But this time they succeeded because they bought Lon Nol, my right arm. My right arm struck out at me before I could defend myself."

The explanation for Lon Nol acting as he did is more complex than that he had been bought up suddenly by the CIA. One could go back to 1952 when a moderately left-wing Democratic Party held such legislative powers as were available in those days of the French protectorate. On June 12 of that year Prime Minister Huy Kanthoul announced the discovery of a plot to overthrow the government and of a cache of arms at the disposal of the plotters who were headed by Lon Nol and Yem Sambour (later to become Lon Nol's foreign minister after the 1970 coup). Both were arrested but released by an intimidated Huy Kanthoul a few days later. That was the first indication of the sort of role Lon Nol hoped to play in an independent Cambodia. But he had to wait another 18 years.

After the Geneva Agreements wrote into international law the attributes of independence which Sihanouk had wrung out of the French eight months earlier, new forces and trends appeared on the Cambodian horizon. Until 1954 there was practically no Cambodian working class, except for the rubber plantation workers; nor was there an indigenous capitalist class. Both classes started to emerge once independence had opened the way for economic development. Two trends appeared. Sihanouk favored the development of state enterprise. Lon Nol, Sirik Matak, Yem Sambour and others were for private, capitalist enterprise. Sihanouk was for state enterprise because he foresaw correctly that private enterprise at that stage of Cambodia's development would have to depend on injections of foreign capital. It would mean that colonialism, thrown out by the front door, would return through the back entrance. With help from the socialist countries, a number of state enterprises were built—textile plants, a cement plant, paper mills, rubber processing industries and others.

Although the nationalized enterprises were nominally run by the state, in fact they were run for the profit of elements of the Cambodian upper and privileged class whose members competed for managerial jobs and the lucrative rake-offs which went with them. State enterprises, even normally profitable ones like textile mills, always ended up with deficits because what should have been profits went into the pockets of the managerial staff. It was similar to bureaucratic capitalism in Kuomintang China. The people paid taxes to finance nominally state enterprises, but the profits went into the pockets of bureaucrats who controlled and managed them. Production for the tax-paying consumers was the least of the worries of the privileged managerial staff. A bureaucratic capitalist class arose as a new element in Cambodian society. But at least it was a national element and, objectively speaking, Sihanouk in defending the country's real independence, defended at the same time the interests of that class.

Lon Nol, Sirik Matak, Yem Sambour and the banker Song Sak, referred to in the previous chapter, favored a compradore-type capitalism dependent on foreign capitalism. Their natural ally and purveyor of capital was the United States and thus they were headed on a collision course with Sihanouk's nationalist concepts. In all fairness it must be stated that Sihanouk's motive in opting for state enterprise as the main line of economic development, was not to create lucrative jobs for corrupt officials. It was to push on with the economic development of the country in such a way as to avoid the risk of the country's hard-won independence being whittled away by foreign economic penetration. His policies brought benefits to the people and, in his way, he was fulfilling the tasks of the national, democratic revolution which orthodox, left-wing forces accepted as appropriate to that stage of Cambodia's social and economic development. There was a steady increase in living standards, irrigation projects for the peasants, and vastly improved public health and educational facilities at the disposal of their children.

Left-wing forces were in somewhat of a dilemma, especially the Pracheachon (People's Party) which was in fact the Cambodian Communist Party, formed after the Indo-Chinese Communist Party was dissolved in 1951 and separate parties were set up in each of the three Indochina states. They supported Sihanouk's policy of independence and neutrality, and also priority for state enterprise. But they also had their historic task of defending the interests of Cambodian workers. This brought them face to face with the problem of how far they should concede on questions of class interests in favor of national interests. The dilemma became the more acute as Sihanouk unquestionably waged a stubborn struggle against U.S. imperialism. Furthermore, his neutralism (after the war started in South Vietnam) represented a precious form of support for the struggle of the Vietnamese people.

Three sorts of antagonisms may be defined:

(1) The people as a whole against the United States and its activities in the area. Progressive forces, including the Pracheachon, considered that the anti-U.S. struggle and the defense of Sihanouk's policy of neutrality and independence was the most important task.

(2) The working people against their employers, in state as well as in private enterprises. The Pracheachon was bound to defend working-class interests but not to the extent where this would weaken the main struggle to defend national independence.

(3) Antagonisms within the ruling class, between the protagonists of national, bureaucratic capitalism and those supporting foreign-dominated, compradore capitalism. This latter antagonism, symbolized by Sihanouk on the one hand and Lon Nol-Sirik Matak on the other, certainly was not seen very clearly by Sihanouk at first. This was at least partly due to the feudal trappings of the past which, despite the fact that Sihanouk stepped down from the throne within a year of independence, had produced something approaching servility in relations between the Chief of State and his Cabinet. Lon Nol was one of those who scrupulously observed the outer form of such relationships, and used these, in fact, to mask his real feelings. (Sihanouk revealed at his Peking press conference that the National Assembly, presided over by Lon Nol, unanimously offered prayers for Sihanouk's health three days before it deposed him!)

For progressives, the antagonisms within the ruling class were expressed in the fact that while Sihanouk welcomed their staunch support for his policies of neutrality, independence and development of the state sector of the economy, they were persecuted by Lon Nol as head of the armed forces and state police. Lon Nol was also particularly zealous in digging up evidence of "subversive activities" by progressive intellectuals and deliberately creating a rift between them and Sihanouk. On one occasion "proof" of a left-wing plot against Sihanouk was supplied to Lon Nol via the U.S. Embassy in Phnom Penh to divert attention from a real CIA-hatched plot earlier the same year.

The position of the Pracheachon, the leadership of which virtually went "underground" after the formation of Sihanouk's party, the Sangkum, was to support Sihanouk's policies but also to prepare for the possibility of his downfall. In discussions with some of their leaders in 1956, I learned that it was their belief that in the long run either Sihanouk would be forced to align himself with the policy of Lon Nol or be eliminated. From that time on the Pracheachon and allied groups began to prepare for the latter eventuality.

As the country and its economy developed, so the antagonisms within the ruling class deepened, especially during those early years when Washington consciously fostered the growth of a pro-U.S. compradore capitalist class by refusing aid for anything other than private enterprise. Antagonisms between the developing working class and their employers also deepened. By 1963 this had led to police repression against progressives whose activities had been too marked. Lon Nol had been very impressed by the military coup in Burma in 1962 in which his opposite number, General Ne Win, had seized power. Rumors were very strong in Phnom Penh in the months that followed that Lon Nol was contemplating the same sort of coup. Sihanouk got wind of this and produced a play in which Lon Nol played the role of a plotter against the Monarchy. It was a device he was to employ several times when antagonisms within the ruling class showed signs of getting out of hand.

In 1963 some progressive intellectuals started to "disappear." Among the first were Son Sen, a principal of Phnom Penh Teachers' Training College, and two professors, Ieng Sary and Salot Sar. They had been marked down for special attention by Lon Nol's police. A year later their wives vanished. Ieng Sary's wife had been head teacher at a Phnom Penh secondary school and was Cambodia's first college graduate in English literature. The rumors in Phnom Penh were that first the husbands, then the wives had been arrested. In fact they were among the first to start organizing resistance bases should these be necessary later. By this time, apart from the threats of internal repression, there were external threats from the United States, already waging "special war" in South Vietnam which threatened to spill across Cambodia's frontiers, as well as specific military threats against Cambodia from the Saigon and Bangkok regimes. The CIA-organized Khmer Serei forces, based at that time mainly in South Vietnam, were working actively and openly for the overthrow of Sihanouk.

This was a period when Sihanouk displayed great skill in what was often referred to as his diplomatic "balancing act" aimed at preserving Cambodian neutrality at all costs and keeping the country as an "oasis of peace" in war-torn Southeast Asia. He strengthened Cambodia's relations with the socialist world, including the establishment of friendly relations with Hanoi. To offset this "opening to the left" he also strengthened relations with capitalist France, the latter sharing Sihanouk's interest in curbing U.S. incursions into what France considered its own sphere of interest in Indochina. By 1965 when the United States committed its combat troops to South Vietnam and started the bombing of the North, Sihanouk had taken a clear position of condemning U.S. aggression in Vietnam, and had established unofficial relations with the National Liberation Front (NLF) of South Vietnam. Sihanouk knew enough about his country's history to understand that friendly relations with Vietnam were essential for Cambodia's survival and he quickly recognized that there were two Vietnams: An aggressive, expansionist Vietnam based in Saigon which would pursue a traditional policy of hostility toward Cambodia, and a progressive, friendly Vietnam based in Hanoi and at the NLF headquarters in the South, with which Cambodia could live in mutually friendly relations.

By May 1965 diplomatic relations with the United States had been severed and relations with the NLF became closer than ever. Sihanouk's great worry was to keep the war from overflowing into Cambodian territory. Cambodia, the NLF and North Vietnam all had an interest in preventing this. Cambodian neutrality—if only the denial of the country to the Americans for military bases—was precious enough support for the NLF in its titanic confrontation with the United States. Progressive forces inside the country gave all-out support to Sihanouk at this time. It coincided with important decrees nationalizing the banks and the import-export trade to weaken the basis of America's natural allies among the compradore-type capitalists. This provoked the start of serious plotting by Lon Nol and Sirik Matak. If Lon Nol had been impressed by General Ne Win's 1962 coup in Burma, he was doubly and trebly impressed by General Suharto's coup in Indonesia in October 1965.

When banker Song Sak fled from Phnom Penh with 400 million riels (equivalent of over $10 million at official exchange rates) the United States lost the head of its CIA organization in Cambodia. Part of his activities, discovered immediately after his flight, was the organization of a network of local CIA agents, lavishly paid from a fund especially established by the CIA in his bank. His anti-state financial manipulations and sabotage of the state-controlled enterprises was discovered by Son Sann, then manager of Cambodia's National Bank. He informed Sihanouk who immediately ordered Song Sak's arrest. But due to conniv-ance with his closest associate, Sirik Matak, the banker made good his escape and went off to become openly what he had been all the time, one of the top three leaders of the Khmer Serei.

"Song Sak tried to buy up those who behaved honestly in the administration," Sihanouk said at his Peking press conference. "He tried to open the gates for U.S. imperialism. He had inexhaustible funds and at the time we could not understand from where they came. Later we had indisputable proof that they came from the CIA."

Not long after Son Sak's flight, Sirik Matak, then ambassador to Peking, asked Sihanouk to transfer him since he was "bored to death" in Peking. He asked specifically to be posted to Japan. Sihanouk agreed and after a period in

Phnom Penh, he went to Tokyo as ambassador in 1966. There he resumed his ties with Song Sak, reestablishing links with the CIA interrupted by the latter's abrupt flight. In referring to the Lon Nol-Sirik Matak plot, Sihanouk said:

"The Americans succeeded because they bought up Lon Nol. This was possible because his 'eminence grise', Sirik Matak, had long flirted with the United States, starting from the time he became ambassador to Japan. He prepared the plot from that time, working out the details with the CIA in Tokyo and later when he was posted as our ambassador to Manila. I do not say the Japanese and Philippine governments were involved. It was the United States, SEATO and the CIA." Sihanouk went on to explain that as Sirik Matak considered himself a claimant to the throne, he had always been hostile: "He could never tolerate me, but he was a childhood friend of Lon Nol. He never cooperated with the government or any National Assembly, except the last one. Later he simply became a U.S. agent."

It seems clear that by the carefully prepared plot to overthrow Sihanouk and all he stood for, the CIA wanted to avoid the cruder sort of Latin America-type coups they had fomented in Laos, and had at first experimented with in Cambodia. Some more "constitutional" methods had to be found. Cambodia was too much in the public eye and Sihanouk's neutralism had won too much international acceptance, and also was too firmly supported inside the country, for a straight-out military coup.

On September 11, 1966 there were general elections for the sixth National Assembly since independence. The results of these elections provided the "constitutional" framework within which the coup could be organized. Sihanouk explained at his Peking press conference that as Sangkum was a fusion of political parties of all tendencies, he, as the Sangkum president, in consultation with other leaders chose candidates to maintain a careful balance within the National Assembly between left, right and center tendencies. "In this way we could maintain stability. But for the last elections, I fell into a CIA trap. The latter financed a monstrous press

. campaign against my so-called 'dictatorship', denouncing the 'single-party system', accusing me of having 'massacred democracy in Cambodia'. We decided not to propose candidates from the top for the 1966 elections, but to permit a 'free for all'.

"The result was confusion. There were sometimes 20 or 30 candidates for each seat. People had no idea whom to choose. The richest of the bourgeoisie, the natural allies of the United States, spent money like water financing electoral campaigns by ultra-rightist, reactionary candidates. Voters received textiles, medicines, free cinema tickets, toys and sweets for their children from these ultra-rightists. Lon Nol used the army and police to intimidate the voters. The people had no way of distinguishing between real and spurious patriots. The result was that only three authentic patriots were elected for the 92 seats contested. But a campaign was organized even against these three and not long afterward, they left for resistance bases in the countryside."

Lon Nol was appointed prime minister of the government which emerged from this ultra-right wing Assembly. Within six months there were serious incidents involving armed suppression of peasants in Battambang province and Lon Nol had "discovered" a left-wing plot to overthrow the government. In fact what happened was a deliberate provocation organized by Lon Nol to provide the background for a Suharto-type coup. Over the years, hundreds of families in Battambang province had carved farms out of virgin land, gradually transforming what had been dense jungle into flourishing fields. Traditionally, in Cambodia, those who clear and cultivate common lands automatically are the owners. In early 1967 Lon Nol's troops arrived and started evicting the peasants, producing papers to show the land belonged to high-ranking government officials. Lon Nol's aim was to rent the farms out to former Khmer Serei troops who were supposed to have "rallied" to the government. It was a strategic area close to the Thai frontier, over the other side of which was the main body of the Khmer Serei and their CIA-run operational bases.

To protest the evictions there were mass demonstrations in Battambang city in which Vietnamese and Chinese residents took part, thus giving Lon Nol the pretext to claim that "Vietminh" and "Maoist" Chinese were responsible. At the beginning of all this Sihanouk was in France for medical attention and Lon Nol sent alarmist reports that the country was about to explode in violent revolution. His troops continued evicting the peasants, confiscating the arms normally possessed by them in that jungle region as protection against wild animals.

Sihanouk returned from France to face, for the first time in his career, a hostile demonstration demanding the resignation of the government, dissolution of the right-wing Assembly and new elections. The press campaign against the three left-wing deputies was stepped up. They were accused of being "Vietcong" and "Maoist" agents.

It is difficult to know how things would have developed had it not been for a most providential accident to Lon Nol at that time. A jeep driven by Lon Nol's long-time rival at the Defense Ministry, General Nhiek Thiou Long, overturned on a steep embankment, pinning Lon Nol underneath. The driver escaped injury but Lon Nol was sufficiently incapacitated to take him out of circulation for many weeks. However, the process he had set in motion in Battambang continued to develop. In April 1967, peasants attacked a military post to retrieve arms that had been seized from them, then disappeared into the forest. A regular military campaign was launched against them, including the use of planes to bomb their jungle hideouts.

Lon Nol resigned at the end of April, ostensibly because of his injuries but more likely because Sihanouk was alarmed by the situation that had developed in the six months during which Lon Nol had been at the helm. Sihanouk appointed a government of "technicians" chosen from outside the National Assembly, including a few progressives.

There was a sensation in Phnom Penh when it became known that at first two of the left-wing deputies, and then the third, had disappeared. These were the economists, Khieu

Samphan and Hou Youn, and the lawyer, Hu Nim—all outstanding intellectuals and each holding a doctorate in his respective specialty. The rumors in Phnom Penh at the time were that they had been arrested, probably killed. In fact, as with the three teachers four years earlier, they had withdrawn to the protection of resistance bases, already well prepared to receive them. This started a movement of literally thousands of young people, many of them students, to the resistance bases in the Elephant mountains in the South, the Cardamomes in the West and the frontier areas with South Vietnam in the Northeast. From that time in late 1967, there were almost daily communiques about clashes between the Khmers Rouges and the forces of "law and order" in widely separated parts of the country. The Khmers Rouges did not launch offensive actions but they defended themselves and consolidated their bases.

Throughout 1968 things moved along uneasily, with Sihanouk gradually withdrawing from effective control of state affairs. In the United States Nixon replaced President Johnson in the White House in January 1969 and soon produced his own version of "disengagement" with the magic formula of the "Vietnamization" of the war. The Lon Nol-Sirik Matak group was delighted with this turn of events because it meant that the United States would not be pulling out of Vietnam after all. Nixon was refusing to concede defeat. Prospects of a nationalist and neutralist coalition government in Saigon which had loomed on the horizon at the Paris peace talks, had now receded. The Lon Nol-Sirik Matak group began to recover from their shocked surprise at the weakness of the U.S.-Saigon forces as displayed during the NLF's 1968 Tet offensive. With Nixon, "Vietnamization," and indefinite continuation of the war, and the maintenance of the Thieu-Ky regime in Saigon, they could push their own pro-American, anti-neutralist policies more openly.

Nixon's advisers had persuaded him that the full success of "Vietnamization" hinged on weakening the NLF sufficiently by striking at their frontier bases to ensure there would be no "come-back" during the American limited withdrawal. Stable pro-Western regimes, which would not be shaken by the reduced U.S. military presence in South Vietnam, must be installed in the "perimeter countries," Laos and Cambodia. Such regimes certainly would cooperate with the U.S.-Saigon Command in sealing off the Cambodian and Laotian frontiers with South Vietnam. The massive use of U.S. air and fire power could take care of the 30-mile gateway from North Vietnam along the Demilitarized Zone. With South Vietnam hermetically sealed off from all supply routes, the Saigon troops, with U.S. air and artillery support, could easily mop up the rest of the NLF forces inside the country.

The attempt to seal off the frontiers with Laos was made in September 1969 by a surprise attack against the Plain of Jars (described in detail in another chapter). Getting rid of Sihanouk was the essential precondition to sealing off the Cambodian frontiers.

In August 1969, the ailing, 64 years-old Penn Nouth, who had been in charge of a caretaker government, had to resign for reasons of serious ill-health. Sihanouk named Lon Nol to replace him and the latter chose Sirik Matak as his deputy premier and also entrusted him with the ministries of the Interior, Security, National Education and Religious Affairs —the latter very important because of the vital role the Buddhist hierarchy plays in Cambodian public life. The following month Lon Nol went to France for "health reasons," leaving the field clear for Sirik Matak as acting prime minister. Previously, in June of that year, diplomatic relations had been resumed with the United States. The stage was now set and the principal actors on the spot for the last act, the overthrow of Sihanouk and his brand of neutralism, which had been a major aim of U.S. policy toward Cambodia for 15 years.

At the end of the year, the National Assembly, at Sirik Matak's initiative annulled various measures of state control over banking and foreign trade, in favor of a "liberalization" of the economy to make the country more "attractive" to foreign investors. Sihanouk vigorously opposed these measures but failed to get National Assembly support. Four ministers, loyal to him, resigned. According to Cambodian parliamentary practice, this should have been enough to bring down the government. Sirik Matak showed no intention of stepping down and his position was reinforced because Lon Nol was out of the country. Sihanouk then urged that the resignation of the four ministers be held in abeyance until Lon Nol's return. But within a few hours Sirik Matak announced in a press communique that he had accepted the resignations. This was the first official action of defiance against the Chief of State. It was in fact a carefully staged mini-coup by the compradore capitalists.

Sihanouk's riposte was to call a National Congress of Sangkum, a device he often employed when he wanted to speak directly to the people and to obtain popular support for his policies. Delegates from all over the country to the National Congress approved his position. Satisfied with this moral victory, Sihanouk together with his wife, elder statesman Penn Nouth and a few other close collaborators, left for medical treatment in France, arriving there on January 10, 1970. It seems his intention was to let Sirik Matak "stew in his own juice" for a while, then to make a leisurely return journey via Paris, Moscow and Peking, coming home with offers of political and economic support from Cambodia's traditional friends—France, the USSR and People's China. Lon Nol came to Rome where Sihanouk had made a brief stop-over to pay his respects and renew assurances of his eternal fidelity.

I visited Phnom Penh during the first half of February 1970, by which time the anti-Vietnamese attacks in certain of the newspapers—said to be receiving generous U.S. subsidies—had reached explosive proportions. They were in sharp contradiction to the officially proclaimed policy of friendship to North Vietnam and the Provisional Revolutionary Government of South Vietnam, both of which by then had embassies in Phnom Penh. The press attacks were paralleled by a whispering campaign launched by some pro-U.S. embassies, recalling historic quarrels between Cambodia and Vietnam and the imperative necessity for Vietnam to push outward into underpopulated countries like Cambodia. The whispering campaign had in fact started about June 1969, just prior to the official visit of Prime Minister Huynh Tan Phat of the Provisional Revolutionary Government of South Vietnam, and had intensified month by month since.

Significant also was the fact that attacks by the U.S.-Saigon armed forces against Cambodian frontier villages had been very much increased since the Nixon administration took over. Among the more serious violations were chemical warfare air raids against Cambodian rubber plantations, one third of which were affected by a systematic attack spread over several days in April 1969. Another was the shelling of Dak Dam village on November 16-17, 1969 in which 25 Cambodians were killed and ten wounded, one of the most serious incidents until then. (The U.S. government later offered $400 compensation to the next-of-kin of those killed!)

One high-ranking Cambodian official whom I met in February 1970 said: "Some people think all this is part of a stick-and-carrot treatment. In fact all we are getting so far is the big stick." But he went on to say that a "carrot" was being promised only when Cambodia had given proof by deeds and not by words that there was a real change of heart toward the United States. World Bank officials arrived during my February visit and I talked with some of them. But they showed an elaborate disinterest in any immediate aid projects. My impression was they were there to reinforce the U.S. Embassy attitude that concrete evidence of a "change of heart" was needed before World Bank money would be available.

It is in this context that the "spontaneous" demonstrations on March 11 and the sacking of the embassies of the Democratic Republic of Vietnam and the Provisional Revolutionary Government of South Vietnam has to be seen. It was significant too that the slogans were posted up in English; that Western correspondents, normally banned from

Cambodia, were on hand, and the embassy sackings were so beautifully filmed that "it looked more like a movie than a documentary," as one top English TV executive remarked to me later. The sacking of the embassies has to be seen also as an organic part of the plot to depose Prince Sihanouk. It was all written into the one scenario, with timing that does credit to the stage managers. The sackings took place just 24 hours after Sihanouk's announcement that Premier Pham Van Dong of North Vietnam would pay a state visit to Cambodia and a few hours before the Head of State was to fly off to Moscow from Paris. His actual overthrow took place a few hours before he was due to leave Moscow for Peking as the last stop on the way home.

The noise about "North Vietnamese and Vietcong" troops was an important element in the scenario which Sihanouk denounced as a diversionary maneuver to cover up the real intentions of the plotters. Sihanouk knew, the Cambodian people knew and, above all, General Lon Nol as former Defense Minister knew, that whatever NLF troops overflowed into the frontier areas from time to time came not with any hostile intent toward Cambodia, but as part of their fight against the common enemy—U.S. aggression. Their target was Saigon, not Phnom Penh.

During the 1969-70 session of the UN General Assembly, Cambodia's delegate, Huot Sambath (who later declared himself for Sihanouk) presented a list of 7,000 violations committed by U.S.-Saigon forces between 1962 and the end of 1969, resulting in over 300 Cambodians killed and over 700 wounded. There had never been any casualties due to the actions or presence of Vietnamese resistance forces in the frontier areas.

There had been many scores of ICC* investigations into U.S.—Saigon frontier violations, especially in the so-called Parrot's Beak area, but despite the most assiduous efforts of

*The International Control Commission, consisting of Canada, India and Poland, which was set up at the Geneva Conference of 1954 to supervise the ceasefire at the end of the first Indochina war.

the Canadian member, no evidence was ever found of any NLF presence to "justify" such violations and massacres of Cambodian villagers in the frontier areas. The victims were always exclusively Cambodians and not Vietnamese. The synthetic indignation worked up over "North Vietnamese" and NLF forces on Cambodian soil was an essential ingredient of the plan to overthrow Sihanouk and for the new Lon Nol-Sirik Matak regime to "prove by deeds a change of heart."

At the time when Cambodia was seriously threatened by simultaneous invasions from South Vietnam and Thailand, with Khmer Serei units ready to follow on the heels of the invaders, Sihanouk and Lon Nol, as Defense Minister, both understood that it was the NLF's control of the main part of South Vietnam's frontiers with Cambodia that enabled Lon Nol to concentrate his troops on the Thai frontier and counter the invasion threat. For a long period it was the NLF that protected Cambodia's eastern frontiers. It was the NLF also which made things so hot for the Khmer Serei in South Vietnam that they had to abandon their bases there and move into Thailand. (In early 1964, I personally handed Sihanouk, as a gift from Nguyen Huu Tho, president of the NLF, a collection of training manuals and operational plans of the Khmer Serei after the NLF had overrun their main base in South Vietnam during my visit to the NLF areas.)

With the deposition of Sihanouk as Head of State, a whole era in Cambodia had come to an end. The question in everyone's minds was, What next? It appears that Washington and some U.S. allies were quite convinced that Sihanouk would accept the blow philosophically and retire, like Bao Dai,* to a villa in the South of France, which the French government quickly assured him would be available. The Cambodian people would accept the new regime at its face value, according to these "experts," and any unrest would

---

*The ex-Monarch of Vietnam under the Japanese and French who retired to the French Riviera in 1955, after being deposed by pro-U.S. dictator Ngo Dinh Diem of South Vietnam.

quickly be diverted into racial outbursts against the Vietnamese and indignation against Sihanouk and the royal family, based on a high-pressure slander campaign. Within a few days after the coup, psychological warfare "experts" had arrived from Indonesia to advise on how to whip up anti-Vietnamese, anti-Communist, anti-Sihanouk campaigns. In connection with the latter, there was a fascinating paragraph in "The Periscope" column of *Newsweek* (May 25, 1970): "A team of Cambodian officers secretly visited Indonesia last November, and again in January, to study in depth how the Indonesian Army managed to overthrow President Sukarno. This, some Indonesians say, gave Djakarta advance knowledge of Cambodian Gen. Lon Nol's coup against Prince Norodom Sihanouk last March. It also helps explain Indonesia's prompt offer to send arms to Lon Nol."

Those, however, who calculated that Norodom Sihanouk would passively accept the *fait accompli* of his overthrow woefully underestimated the character of Sihanouk and the qualities of the Cambodian people.

5

Sihanouk Fights Back

In a car on the way to Moscow airport for a plane that was to take him to Peking, Sihanouk learned from Soviet Prime Minister Alexei Kosygin that he had been deposed. Members of his entourage knew of it some hours earlier but could not decide how to break the news. It came as a complete shock. There had been no warning at all. But Sihanouk's reaction was immediate—and predictable to those who really knew him. He would fight back. On the plane to Peking he was already planning the counterattack; on arrival, he was immediately assured of Chinese support by his old friend Chou En-lai who met him at the airport. A few days later he received the same assurances from Premier Pham Van Dong of North Vietnam who made a special visit to Peking—secret at the time—for that purpose. By March 23, five days after the coup, Sihanouk had formulated a five-point proclamation which will remain an historic landmark in Sihanouk's own evolution and as opening a new chapter in Cambodian history. In his capacity of Head of State, Sihanouk:

Accused the Lon Nol regime of high treason and decreed its dissolution.

Announced that a Government of National Union would be formed.

Called for the setting up of a consultative assembly formed from the broadest sections of the community, including "all patriotic, progressive and anti-imperialist tendencies."

Called for the creation of a National Liberation Army to fight against U.S. imperialism and its agents inside the country.

Called for the creation of a National United Front for the liberation of the country and to handle the tasks of reconstruction after victory was won.

He appealed to his compatriots to make their choice, to rise up and overthrow the Lon Nol-Sirik Matak regime.

Things began to move rapidly after that—more rapidly than Sihanouk could have imagined at the moment of the coup. Vitally important was the immediate response of progressive intellectuals to his appeal. It had been broadcast over Peking and Hanoi radios, monitored and recorded on tape inside Cambodia and rebroadcast from thousands of loudspeakers all over the country. The effect of Sihanouk's voice—and on such a theme—was electrifying. Lon Nol had nothing with which to counter. He had prepared most carefully the military side of his coup, and the political intrigue which accomplished it. But he had done nothing to prepare public opinion. His slander campaign against Sihanouk's private life could not have moved people less. They were interested in basic questions of peace and war, independence, defense against foreign invasions.

Within 24 hours, there was a joint declaration of support from the three missing left-wing deputies—Hou Youn, Hu Nim and Khieu Samphan—the first news of them for almost three years. The fact that these outstanding intellectuals, pioneers of the resistance struggle within the country with high prices on their heads, offered all-out support to Sihanouk had a galvanizing effect on progressives inside and outside the country. The three had suffered greatly during the previous four years. But they showed their maturity in deciding that policies and not personalities counted. Sihanouk had laid down a correct line—they were prepared to forget the past, accept that line for the present and fight for the future. In their analysis of the situation, contained in their statement of support, they made it clear that Sihanouk's appeal corresponded precisely to the new phase of the national democratic revolution. Even the most orthodox of left-wing progressives could support it, as they did.

"We unreservedly support the March 23 declaration made in Peking by the Head of State, Prince Norodom Sihanouk," states the deputies' declaration. "We appeal to all our compatriots in the towns as in the countryside not to enroll as cannon fodder in the army or police of the American imperialists and those national traitors, Lon Nol and Sirik Matak; not to pay them any taxes or respect their barbarous laws; to unite sincerely and closely in the Cambodian National United Front; to organize guerrilla units and armed forces to fight against and overthrow their regime and set up honest administrations at hamlet, village, district and provincial levels." The deputies appealed to soldiers and civil servants to support the people in their struggle and to join the ranks of the resistance forces. They referred to the broad international support the resistance movement was bound to receive "especially from the Vietnamese and Laotian peoples" in their struggle for national liberation.

When did any resistance movement get off to a more auspicious start? Unity of a broad spectrum of forces from peasants and workers to the monarchy! Resistance bases already formed, six main ones dominating all key areas of the country. The embryo of a liberation army and leaders tempered by three years of underground struggle—plus veterans of the anti-Japanese and anti-French resistance. Arms in abundance, available immediately after Sihanouk's appeal.

In the past, the NLF of South Vietnam did not supply arms to the Khmers Rouges resistance fighters, although they had abundant stocks in the frontier areas. They did not want to do anything which might endanger Sihanouk's neutrality. They loyally respected agreements on non-interference in each other's internal affairs. The Khmers Rouges, once they went over to armed resistance in 1967, were something of an embarrassment, in fact, to the NLF. The latter could not appeal to them, in the higher interest of aiding the NLF to defeat U.S. imperialism, to call off their own struggle. But it was easy for Lon Nol to persuade Sihanouk, as he did at one period, that it was the Vietcong who were behind the Khmers

Rouges and it became a very delicate problem for the NLF to handle. Fortunately, the main bases and centers of armed struggle were remote from the border areas of South Vietnam. To the best of my knowledge, the only help given the Cambodian resistance fighters was when a group, hard-pressed by Lon Nol's troops in the frontier areas, occasionally would be allowed to slip through NLF positions to be passed back into Cambodian territory as soon as possible, perhaps in some other sector.

With Sihanouk's appeal the situation was transformed. He called for a "struggle waged in common with other anti-imperialist, people's forces of fraternal countries." If the Americans were somewhat disappointed that many of the arms caches uncovered during their invasion of Cambodian territory were empty, they should have looked for the missing arms in the hands of tens of thousands of Cambodian resistance fighters, distributed in the very first days following Sihanouk's appeal for armed struggle.

Large-scale spontaneous uprisings took place immediately after Sihanouk's appeal. Although Lon Nol tried to pretend these were launched by the "Vietnamese" and instigated a series of savage massacres against the Vietnamese community which shocked the world, journalists on the spot confirmed that it was Cambodians and not Vietnamese who turned out in massive demonstrations against the regime; that it was Cambodians and not Vietnamese whose corpses choked the roads and whose wounded filled the provincial hospitals. Hundreds of people were killed between March 26 and 28 along the road leading from Cambodia's third largest town of Kompong Cham to the capital, many of them shot down in the outskirts of Phnom Penh itself. Referring to the Kompong Cham incidents, correspondent J.C. Pomonti wrote in *Le Monde* (March 31, 1970):

"The demonstrators (about 3,000 according to an eye-witness) were spread all over town and along the road, stopping vehicles and painting 'Long Live Sihanouk' on the doors and distributing the Prince's portrait to the drivers. After that, and in circumstances not precisely known, a convoy of about 50 trucks and cars, overflowing with demonstrators, including a lot of students and high school pupils, formed up and set out for Phnom Penh, about 60 miles to the South. At Koki, about 12 miles to the west of the capital, incidents had taken place on the Thursday night and early Friday morning. According to a Cambodian parachute officer, a lot of Vietnamese 'disguised as peasants with a few arms' had infiltrated villages of the area.''

The report goes on to refer to "peasants armed with knives'' who attacked a government office in Takeo province, burning all files they could lay their hands on. Pomonti quotes a local official as saying that he was having great difficulty in "explaining things to the peasants.'' He refers to armed clashes at the approach to a bridge less than a mile from the center of Phnom Penh and at road junctions on the outskirts of the city. All these demonstrations were by Cambodians not Vietnamese. Pomonti quotes the Takeo official as saying: "In my district there are very few Vietnamese and they are very careful not to budge.''

"This is Sihanouk country, its people fanatically loyal to the prince who was deposed as chief of state ten days ago," wrote Jack Foisie of the Los Angeles *Times* from Kompong Cham (as reported in the *International Herald Tribune*, March 31, 1970). "Mobs beat and stomped to death two representatives of the National Assembly who returned here to explain to their constituents why they had voted to oust Norodom Sihanouk. In retaliation, army troops rode into town and shot into a crowd Friday morning, killing 26 persons—by the provincial governor's count—and wounding 62. . . . The province . . . appeared to be in turmoil.

"Villagers stuck pictures of Sihanouk in our face and asked in guttural French if we were for him. They backed up their fury with machetes, sharp farm tools and clubs. A few were armed with French and Czech rifles. We nodded our assent and they pounded our backs and whooped us on our way.

"The provincial governor, Tian Kien Chieng put the number of 'misguided' Cambodians in his area at between 20,000 and 40,000, mostly peasants who he said had come under the influence of North Vietnamese or Cambodian

Communist agents." Foisie quoted the governor as saying the demonstrators "wanted the dissolution of the National Assembly and the restoration of Prince Sihanouk." Previously, resistance leader Hu Nin had been the deputy for Kompong Cham province, reelected in 1966 despite the right-wing pressures and corruption of voters.

These were genuine, spontaneous uprisings of the Cambodian people. Journalists on the spot tended to report only those that took place in the provinces adjacent to Phnom Penh, especially in the sensitive areas between the capital and the South Vietnamese frontier. But in fact they took place all over the country. After several hundred peasants had been slaughtered in Kompong Cham, Takeo, Svay Rieng, Kandal and other provinces in the great wave of spontaneous demonstrations at the end of March, Sihanouk advised against such unarmed actions in favor of organized armed resistance. Thousands of villagers who had fled into the jungle looking for resistance leaders, were contacted, given arms, and advised to return to their villages and set up resistance organizations, including elected committees and self-defense guerilla units.

Thousands of Lon Nol's troops either joined the resistance forces or gave their arms to the resistance and returned to their native villages. In numerous cases they simply piled up their weapons in their barracks and sent word to local resistance leaders to come and collect them. In the Battambang area in the West, an old resistance cadre heard Sihanouk's appeal and without awaiting further instructions he went to talk things over with a company of Lon Nol's troops in his area. They followed him into the jungle where they set up an important resistance base, reinforced a few days later by groups of students from Battambang University. At Siem Reap, near the famous Angkor ruins, students also left *en masse* for the nearest resistance base. Lon Nol's army and administration showed signs of collapsing everywhere, except in the capital itself where the regime could concentrate sufficient armed strength to stabilize the situation. But the army had no stomach for a fight.

At the Neak Luong ferry crossing on the Mekong, 60 miles east of Phnom Penh, the resistance fired a few shots and the defending battalion fled to a Buddhist pagoda, with the resistance forces in pursuit. Bonzes in the pagoda persuaded the troops to lay down their arms and leave. This was how the ferry crossing was captured. (It was recaptured later by Saigon naval-borne troops with U.S. air support.) Of Lon Nol's original 50 battalions, ten had simply dispersed during the first month of action, ten more had been wiped out, surrendered or had crossed over voluntarily to the resistance forces, and another nine were tied down on fixed guard duty. Another 35 battalions of green recruits were formed from bewildered students and others—and acted mainly as arms suppliers to the resistance forces. By the end of the first six weeks, the original six resistance bases had linked up, a regular Liberation Army had been organized at battalion strength with better arms, weapon for weapon, than those of Lon Nol's troops. They were supplemented by regional troops at company level and by self-defense guerrillas in over a hundred villages, both armed equally as well as Lon Nol's troops—armed in fact with the latter's weapons. It was the troops of the Cambodian Liberation Army—not "Vietcong" and "North Vietnamese"—who had liberated most of Cambodia by the time Nixon decided to strike across the frontiers with U.S. troops and send Saigon forces on an operation of the most flagrant aggression to try and wrest back control of Cambodian towns and villages from Cambodian patriots.

The shock troops used by Lon Nol in the very first days after the takeover, and for the massacres of Cambodian peasants and unarmed Vietnamese prisoners, were from the CIA private army of Khmer Serei. During 1969, there were mysterious large-scale defections—entire companies and even battalions—of Thailand-based Khmer Serei mercenaries to the Cambodian government. In one day, 700 crossed the border from Thailand and gave themselves up. Credit for these "defections" was given to Lon Nol. The "deserters," given cash rewards, settled on the land in strategic frontier areas. Phnom Penh sources maintain that they were reformed into units, armed and brought secretly to the capital on the eve of the coup. Their numbers were swelled by hundreds of others, detained in prison and released by Lon Nol within a few days of the coup. Trained killers, with no ties with the country or people to restrain them—they had been recruited from among the Khmer minority in South Vietnam—rapists and looters, the Kmer Serei sowed terror wherever they appeared. The Lon Nol-Sirik Matak coup was the day for which they had been trained. They performed for the CIA the same role as the Vang Pao mercenaries in Laos (described in a later chapter).

On April 24 and 25, 1970 a Summit Conference of the Indochinese Peoples was held "in a locality of the Laos-Vietnam-China" border area. The Cambodian delegation was headed by Prince Sihanouk; the Laotian by Prince Souphanouvong, president of the Lao Patriotic Front; the South Vietnamese delegation by Nguyen Huu Tho, president of the NLF of South Vietnam; and the North Vietnamese by Prime Minister Pham Van Dong. The essence of the agreement reached dealt with the current tasks of uniting to fight an expanded war in Indochina, the principles of applying this unity, and the basis of future relations between the various components. It is a wise and moderate document which affirms that the fundamental positions of the three peoples have not been modified because of the extension of the war. Thus:

"The Cambodian, Lao and South Vietnamese parties affirm that their combat objectives are independence, peace, neutrality, the prohibition of the presence of all foreign troops or military bases on their soil, non-participation in any military alliance, prohibition of the use of their territories by any foreign country for the purpose of aggression against other countries. . . . The people of the Democratic Republic of Vietnam fully respect these legitimate aspirations and unreservedly support the struggle for these lofty objectives."

In other words, despite the greatly changed situation, neutrality remains, with all the implications for an autonomous South Vietnam as a partner in a neutral zone together with Laos and Cambodia.

The principle of the autonomy of each of the components —even while cooperating in military affairs—is clearly stressed in a passage which states: "Proceeding from the principle that the liberation and the defense of each country are the business of each people, the various parties pledge to do all they can to give one another reciprocal support according to the desire of the party concerned and on the basis of mutual respect." There is a further reference to "mutual support in the struggle against the common enemy and to lasting future cooperation in the building of each country according to its own way." Further, "The parties affirm that all problems arising in the relations between the three countries can be solved through negotiations in a spirit of mutual respect, mutual understanding and mutual assistance."

There is no mention of setting up a joint military command, which might have been expected, but there is provision for future meetings at summit level when the occasion requires. It is noted also that the situation for a common struggle is "more favorable than ever" and that the Indochinese peoples "have forged an indestructible solidarity; moreover, as never before they possess considerable forces."

Chou En-lai, who presumably acted as "host" to the conference, gave a banquet after the closing session at which he noted, among other things, that "Under the heavy blows of the three Indochinese peoples and the people of the rest of the world, U.S. imperialism is beset with difficulties both at home and abroad." He promised "powerful backing for the three Indochinese peoples . . . the vast expanse of China's territory is their reliable rear area." Chairman Mao Tse-tung, in one of his rare declarations on international affairs, gave full support to Sihanouk, the joint statement of the Indochina people's summit conference, and the newly established Royal Government of National Union of Cambodia.

Underlining a similar concern on the part of the Soviet Union, Premier Alexei Kosygin on May 4, at his first press conference in six years as prime minister, warned the United States of the consequences of its aggression against Cambodia and launched an urgent appeal for the "unity of all

peace-loving forces" to halt the aggression. In the harshest
language used from Moscow against a President of the United
States since World War II, the declaration read by Premier
Kosygin warned Nixon that the Soviet government would
"draw the appropriate conclusions" for its own future policy
toward the United States. In the light of the aggression
against Cambodia and the "flagrant divorce between the
declarations and assurances of President Nixon and his deeds
in the field of foreign policy," Kosygin asked, "what is the
value of international agreements to which the United States
is, or intends to be, a party if it so unceremoniously violates
its obligations?" In his reply to questions Kosygin characterized the summit conference of the peoples of Indochina as a
"factor of unity" in the fight against U.S. aggression.

6

The New Resistance Government

The summit conference and the clearly defined future roles of the participants cleared the way for a National Congress of the Cambodian People held at the beginning of May, in Peking. Delegates were appointed by the leadership of the resistance in Cambodia in consultation with patriotic Cambodians abroad, including of course Sihanouk in Peking. It was this Congress which drew up the Political Program of the Cambodian National United Front (NUF), confirmed Sihanouk as president, chose an 11-member Political Bureau for the NUF and appointed a Royal Government of National Union, with Penn Nouth as prime minister.

There was considerable applause at the press conference when Sihanouk announced that the three deputies in the resistance had been given key ministries in the government. Khieu Samphan, 40 years old, was named Minister of Defense; Hou Youn, 42, Minister of the Interior, Rural Reforms and Cooperatives; Hu Nim, 41, Minister of Information and Propaganda. Chosen as foreign minister was 48-years-old Sarin Chhak, former Cambodian ambassador to Cairo. The ministry of Public Works, Telecommunications and Reconstruction went to 42-years-old Huot Sambath, former head of Cambodia's delegation to the UN. The youngest member of the Cabinet is 36-years-old Chan Youran, former ambassador to Senegal, and the oldest is Prime Minister Penn Nouth at 64.

The average age of the 12-member cabinet is 48—which happens also to be the age of Sihanouk. It is a young but distinguished government with a high proportion of known patriots and progressives. Next to Sihanouk no one has more prestige inside the country than Penn Nouth whose whole life has been devoted to obtaining and defending Cambodian independence. All 12 members have been ministers or state secretaries in previous governments, two of them ministers of defense—Major General Duong Sam Ol who was defense minister in the last government before that of Lon Nol, and Lieutenant General Hgo Hou who had also been Chief of Staff of the Armed Forces and head of the Air Force. The list included also two former foreign ministers—as minister of Economy and Finance, 44-years-old Thiounn Mumm, Dr. Sc., a well-known progressive who had been in self-imposed exile in France; and 40-years-old Chea San, at present ambassador in Moscow, as minister of Justice and Legal Reforms. Chau Seng, 42, former vice-president of the National Assembly and Sihanouk's one-time dynamic and highly efficient personal secretary, was appointed minister in charge of Special Missions.

There are no members of comparable qualities in Lon Nol's government.

The political program provides for Buddhism remaining as the state religion but freedom for other religions is guaranteed; also the protection of "legitimate rights and interests of foreign nationals who respect our laws and customs." Among social reforms promised are some that will be welcomed with enthusiasm by the peasants, including "Guaranteeing the peasants the right of ownership of the land they cultivate . . . helping the peasants resolve the agrarian problem through a fair solution of unreasonable debts." Other measures deal with revising the system of land rents and interest on loans, exorbitant in some parts of the countryside. These latter measures do not have to await victory in the liberation struggle. They are being applied immediately in scores of liberated villages all over the country.

Polygamy is to be abolished and "effective equality for both sexes" is to be introduced. The type of balance which already existed between the state and private sectors of industry and commerce is to be maintained, as is the nationalization of banks and foreign trade, but with measures aimed at eliminating the type of corruption that crippled state enterprises in the past.

The policy of neutrality is reaffirmed in the section dealing with foreign policy: "Cambodia is ready to make concerted efforts with Laos and Vietnam to make Indochina genuinely a zone of independence, peace and neutrality wherein each nation preserves its integral sovereignty." In general, there is little in the program to cause anxiety to any country except those with aggressive intentions against Cambodia. It is a program capable of rallying the widest support within the country and is in conformity with the strictest principles of peaceful coexistence.

In presenting the program, Sihanouk said it was drawn up and the government was chosen without his participation. "I merely helped correct the French draft of the various documents and a few typing errors," he said, but added that he wholeheartedly approved the decisions. "Our armed forces exist already. The enemy says it is the 'Vietcong' or 'Vietminh' that is liberating our territory. It is not true; it is our own Liberation Army. We lacked a government—now we have a government. We have an administration on the spot. Every time we liberate a village or locality we install the legitimate administration with the difference that now the new political program is being applied—to the great advantage of the people."

As to why the title "*Royal* Government of National Union" is used, Sihanouk explained that it was a question of defending the legitimacy of the regime which he headed and which was established under a Constitution drawn up in 1947, with the participation of all political parties, including the Communist Party, existing at that time. Sihanouk quoted extensively from that Constitution to prove without any shadow of doubt that the coup of March 18, 1970 was a violation of the Constitution and the plotters were guilty of high treason. He also explained, correctly, that although the form of the regime was monarchic, the content was republican from the time he abdicated the throne. But he and the leaders of the National United Front attached great importance to defending the constitutional legitimacy of their government, in contrast to the "illegitimacy" of that headed by Lon Nol, Cheng Heng and Sirik Matak.

In an interview which Sihanouk accorded me on May 6, the day after the formation of the government, and which was filmed and recorded in the garden of the sumptuous, modern palace the Chinese government had put at his disposal as his residence and secretariat, I asked whether the fact that he was in exile in Peking and the government had been formed abroad, did not cut him off from the resistance inside the country. Sihanouk, whom I found "fighting fit," very confident, very militant and vital, replied in English:

"No. We formed the government in response to a request from inside the country, mainly from those in the resistance movement. Leading members of the government, as you know, are actually directing that resistance movement. We can say that our government is not rooted here but is rooted in the soil of Cambodia. I am most anxious to return but the *maquisards* at the resistance bases have told me that I have to fulfill some duties abroad in the international diplomatic field, helpful to the cause of our people in Cambodia." He explained that in matters such as which minister should return and when, only the ministers directing the struggle on the spot had powers to decide. The rest of the government were bound by their decisions in such matters.

At the time of the interview, People's China, North Korea and Cuba had already recognized the government and he had assurances of recognition from about 20 countries in all, not including the Soviet Union or East European countries apart from Albania, Rumania and Yugoslavia. But Sihanouk was confident the Soviet Union would also recognize and after that the rest of the European socialist states.

As to his reaction to the invasion by U.S.-Saigon troops, Sihanouk said: "It does not surprise me because the aim of the March 18 coup was to open the doors of independent and neutral Cambodia to American invasion and occupation.

Because of their 'falling domino' theory, they wanted to occupy Cambodia to strengthen other dominoes and prevent them from falling."

On the previous day President Nixon had given as one of the reasons for the invasion that the United States was "defending Cambodian neutrality." I asked Sihanouk what he thought about that:

"Since President Nixon decided to defend our neutrality," he replied, "Cambodian neutrality no longer exists and our independence has been wiped out. But for the armed intervention of the United States and their satellite invaders, we should be in Phnom Penh and not in Peking. Lon Nol in fact invited them in not to protect the neutrality of Cambodia but to defend his shaky regime."

I asked for his comment on the reason given by the Americans for invading Cambodia, also for the coup, namely the presence of Vietnamese resistance forces on Cambodian soil.

"Before, we were independent," he replied. "We had our neutrality. Now we are a colony of the Americans and we are occupied by 65,000 South Vietnamese troops, mercenaries of the Americans. I was deposed on March 18, because it was said that I allowed 'Vietcong' and 'Vietminh' to occupy Cambodia. They sometimes did come to Cambodia because of some necessity, some strategic or tactical necessity. But this was within the framework of their fight against the United States, to liberate their homeland. Even if they were in Cambodia, they looked toward Saigon. All their efforts were directed toward Saigon and South Vietnam. They wanted to liberate South Vietnam. They never looked in our direction. They recognized *de jure* our frontiers. Even in the future, after their victory, they cannot change the frontiers of Cambodia.

"They are not a threat to Cambodia. But, on the contrary, the Saigon government is a threat to Cambodia since they refuse to recognize our frontiers because they want to take some provinces away from us—Svay Rieng, for instance, which they are now occupying with the forces of General Do

Cao Tri. They also want to take some of the off-shore islands away from us."

Sihanouk also gave his evaluation of the Indochinese peoples summit conference:

"Before the arrival of the French colonialists so-called Indochina did not exist. There was Annam, Tonking, Cochin-China (the three states of Vietnam), Laos and Cambodia. It was France that created Indochina and united us inside a Federation. But our three peoples wanted to win back from the French national independence for our homelands. They had to be in solidarity with each other in order to develop their growing struggle and claims for independence.

"When the Japanese militarists and fascists came into Cambodia during World War II, our three peoples also had to resist this Japanese invasion. So this created, right at the beginning, right at the starting point—many years ago—a solidarity of the peoples of Indochina. That solidarity certainly was greatly strengthened by the American invasion of Indochina, of South Vietnam in particular. But now, U.S. aggression is not only against South Vietnam, but against North Vietnam, against Cambodia and Laos. We have to fight, we have to liberate our countries.

"Conscious of our weaknesses, small peoples who have to fight against a giant, a very big power, with enormous military strength, it is vital for us to unite our efforts, to cooperate closely with each other in order to win. If we want victory, this is what we have to do. It may take a long time. But we are optimistic as far as the victory of our people is concerned."

At his press conference the previous day Sihanouk had also referred to the question of cooperation between the peoples of Indochina: "It is our sacred right to unite with the fraternal Laotian and Vietnamese peoples," he said, and went on to speak about Arabs of widely differing social regimes who were united against Israel. "Because we unite in this struggle, this does not mean we have to become communist satellites or accept foreign invasions. During World War II,

Britain went into and through France to fight the common enemy. No one accused Britain of 'invading France'. We are at home in Indochina. The only foreign invaders are the Americans and their satellites. They should withdraw. They must withdraw, otherwise we will wipe them out. . . . The summit conference has formally declared that Cambodia is to be free of foreign troops. . . . Neither the United States, Australia, South Korea, Thailand or anyone else has the right to come into our Indochina and make war."

Without setting up any formal joint military staff, it appeared that coordinated activity between the Cambodian, Laotian and South Vietnamese resistance forces had developed even before the summit conference. A large liberated area had already been carved out by mid-May in what is known as the "three frontiers area" where Cambodia, Laos and South Vietnam meet. Pathet Lao victories in the Attopeu-Saravane area of the strategic Bolovens Plateau coincided with Cambodian Liberation Army advances in the adjoining northernmost province of Stung Treng, culminating with the capture of the provincial capital of the same name. On the South Vietnamese side NLF control of the Central Highlands extends to the outskirts of Pleiku, with solidly liberated areas to the north and south of that city. Whatever the ebb and flow of battle produces, the peoples of Indochina now have a vast, contiguous and relatively secure base area, linked by territories long since liberated by the Pathet Lao and NLF which are contiguous with North Vietnam and thus with China. In case Thailand intervenes too flagrantly in the affairs of Laos and Cambodia—as she shows every intention of doing—it is predictable that the Pathet Lao, with or without North Vietnamese support, and the Cambodian resistance forces will extend the areas under their control to most of the areas bordering on Thailand. Contact with the Thai liberation forces is facilitated by the fact that Northeast Thailand, where resistance is most active, is populated mainly by people of Lao ethnic origin. In Cambodia, the Cardamomes mountains near the Thai border is one of the oldest and most solid bases of the resistance in that country.

While the U.S.-Saigon Command was piling up "Vietcong body count" figures from Cambodian civilians, massacred by murderous air assaults in the "Parrot's Beak" and "Fishhook" areas of Cambodia; while their ground forces were rushing around to find a "Vietcong Pentagon" to give Nixon some desperately needed justification for his catastrophic military-political blunder, the general staffs of the resistance forces of the three peoples of Indochina were quietly establishing and consolidating common bases for what they all realize will be another protracted phase in their long struggle for independence. What Nixon had counted on as a surprise attack to snatch a quick military victory out of the quagmire in South Vietnam has, in fact, created the conditions for a complete victory of all the peoples of Indochina. At least that is how their leaders see it and they have very sober, logical arguments, based on the recent history of their respective countries to justify their predictions.

No responsible Cambodian, Laotian or Vietnamese leader with whom I have spoken has ever suggested submitting the Cambodian people to the sufferings and sacrifices entailed by a prolonged armed struggle against the most powerful and ruthless armed forces history has known. It was not the Cambodian, Laotian or Vietnamese resistance leaders who tore down the barriers that brought the war cascading over onto Cambodian soil. Once it was done, the Cambodian people had no other choice than to take to arms, as they have done throughout their history, against foreign invaders.

The U.S. method of waging war—to destroy what cannot be occupied—makes it certain that other Cambodian towns will suffer the fate of those like Snoul, Memot, Krek and others in the border areas which were blasted out of existence. Thousands of Cambodian women, old people and children are going to be slaughtered to make up "Vietcong" and eventually "Khmercong" body-count figures. But the resistance will go on as long as a single invader remains on Cambodian soil, on Laotian soil or on Vietnamese soil.

The destruction of material values in Indochina is matched by the destruction of moral values within the United States.

For this eventually there will be an awful day of reckoning for President Nixon or whoever succeeds him in the White House. The rape of Cambodia is just too much for the human conscience. The military and political miscalculations of the U.S. warmakers reflect the total contempt they have for human beings and human values, their total contempt for Cambodian people as for their own people. Despite the computerized soundings of public opinion, nothing seems to have prepared Nixon for the shock waves of revulsion that swept the whole world, including especially the United States, at the horror that the Cambodian invasion represents and at the daily presidential lies of attempted justification.

In a warning to the Lon Nol regime on May 25, the Soviet government, in what many believed the first step toward recognition of Sihanouk's Government of National Union, issued a statement condemning the invasion of Cambodia by U.S.-Saigon troops as a "gross violation of the 1954 agreements on Indochina and of the generally recognized norms of international law. . . . The flame of war has swept Cambodia leaving ruins and ashes where towns and villages had stood and taking toll of the lives of thousands of innocent victims," the statement continued and went on to warn of the possibility of a long civil war. The Soviet would "draw appropriate conclusions" from the choice that the Lon Nol regime would make—"a return to the road of peace and neutrality or unity with the forces of aggression and war."

If he still had any capacity for being moved by international reactions President Nixon should have been particularly hurt when the congress of the West German ruling Social Democrat Party approved a resolution on May 12 condemning the American invasion.

It is not however the reactions of a Nixon or a Lon Nol to international opinion that is decisive in Indochina. It is the struggle of the peoples of Indochina—the peoples of Cambodia, of Vietnam and of Laos.

Part II
Laos

1

Laos and its Problems

On a map of Asia, Laos makes a poor showing as far as geographical size is concerned—like Britain on a map of Europe to the Urals. In fact, Laos is almost exactly the same size as the United Kingdom, a difference of only 28 square miles in favor of Laos. But whereas Britain is very densely populated, Laos is one of the most sparsely populated countries in Asia, about three inhabitants per square mile. It is sometimes described as a large country with few people and especially few Laotians, because the ethnic minorities of the highlands are generally thought to outnumber those who are considered the real Laotians, the plains-dwelling Lao Lum.

Ethnic groupings, customs, types of agricultural pursuits and methods of cultivation vary according to the geographic location of the villages. Those situated on the crests and summits of the mountains and on the plateaus which dominate the least populated areas of the country concentrate on cattle breeding and opium production and also grow maize. On the slopes and hillsides, with the most backward socio-economic formation, the semi-nomadic inhabitants pursue the slash-and-burn system of agriculture under which a patch of forest is hacked out of the mountain slope and burned; hillside rice and maize is then planted in holes poked into the ash-covered earth with a stick, the tribal group moving from one mountain slope to another, returning to original patches only when the forest had covered them again. In the more densely populated fertile plain through which runs the Mekong river, or in the plentiful valleys which shelter its tributaries, the Lao Lum are essentially rice-growers, dependent on seasonal rainfalls.

An exact figure is hard to establish for the population of Laos. An iniquitous head-tax system introduced by the French and which included such refinements as a breast-tax on pregnant women, encouraged the Laotians to conceal the exact number of family adherents and to discourage census-taking. Pregnant women tended to stay away from the markets and other public places. This was especially true among the ethnic minorities whose forests, mountains and difficult access routes facilitated concealment of family details from the tax assessors. Until very recently—in certain regions even still today—tribal and clan conceptions still exist, with elements of slavery and serfdom, of pre-feudal forms of society together with their appropriate forms of family and social organizations, including polyandry.

Among more than 30 different nationalities, the greatest single ethnic grouping and also the most advanced is the Lao Lum of Thai origin, who probably number about one million. The Lao Theung tribes of Indonesian origin, living on the slopes, comprise the largest single minority grouping. Next in importance are the Lao Xung of Chinese origin, among whom the Meo tribes are predominant. They occupy the mountain tops, the women taking care of the crops and cattle, the men redoubtable hunters with crossbows and homemade rifles. In the town and villages of the plains and main communication routes, there are also many Vietnamese of more recent origin, including families of officials brought in by the French to serve in the colonial administration. The Vietnamese in Laos live more or less integrated with the Lao Lum as artisans, shopkeepers, rice farmers and fishermen.

Long before the advent of French colonialism brought the Cambodian and Laotian people together with the Vietnamese in the French colony of Indochina, they were linked by history and Buddhism. A century before the abandonment of the Angkor capital, a young Laotian prince had taken refuge there. His name was Fa Ngoun,* a convert to Buddhism at a

*Sometimes spelt Fa Ngum or Fa Ngun, according to the transcription from Sanskrit.

time when the latter was still competing with Hinduism for acceptance as the main religion in that corner of Asia. In the mid-14th century, Fa Ngoun left Angkor with his most precious possession, a 500-years-old golden statue (or Prabang) of Buddha, reputedly from Ceylon, the very cradle of the Buddhist faith. He established himself hundreds of miles to the north, on the Mekong river at a place then known as Muong Swa, later renamed Luang Prabang (Town of the Golden Buddha). Deeply influenced by his sojourn at Angkor, Prince Fa Ngoun gradually transformed Luang Prabang into a Buddhist center, the precious relic a pole of attraction for bonzes and scholars, the town itself attracting craftsmen and merchants and other elements similar to those that had contributed to the rich life of Angkor.

Once having consolidated his position at Luang Prabang, Fa Ngoun turned his attention to the neighboring principalities of Houa Phan, Muong Phouan (today's Xieng Khouang), Vientiane and Champassac, often at war with each other and their neighbors. When he had subdued them by force of arms or threat of such force, Fa Ngoun, in 1353, founded the Kingdom of Lan Xang (Kingdom of the Million Elephants), with the royal capital at Luang Prabang and Buddhism as the official religion, the whole forming the Kingdom of Laos much as it exists today. Fa Ngoun was succeeded 20 years later by his son who took the name of Sam Sen Thai (Three Hundred Thousand Thai) because a population census conducted by him had yielded 300,000 young men of military age.

The American journalist Arthur J. Dommen, who did considerable research into Laotian history of that period, writes: "The two successive kings, father and son, ruled over a group of vassal princes and exacted recognition from neighboring emperors and potentates. Their source of power was a centralized standing army of 150,000 men, divided into infantry, cavalry and elephant corps, supported by a supply corps of 20,000 coolies. In practice, each of the local governors exerted considerable control over the soldiers recruited from his district, who also served as the local police force. With this machinery of state, the two kings preserved the independence of Lan Xang from enemies without and dissolution within."*

Despite waves of internal dissensions and foreign invasions—the Siamese and Burmese from the West, the Annamites from the East—the kingdom founded by Fa Ngoun lasted some 350 years and in a modest way corresponded to the Golden Age of Cambodia's Angkorian period. If no great temples were built, the country was covered liberally with Buddhist pagodas and enjoyed peace and relatively stable government. In the 16th century, the reigning King Sathatharit transferred the royal capital downstream to Vientiane, the present administrative capital of Laos, apparently because of the danger to Luang Prabang from Burmese invaders whom Sathatharit had twice defeated.

The first westerners—Jesuit missionaries and a group of Dutch traders, headed by Gerrit van Wuystoff—arrived in the mid-17th century, during the reign of King Souligna Vongsa (1637-94). They seemed to have found the Laotians much as they are today (when they are not being bombed or shot at)—gentle, peaceful, easy-going people, generous and hospitable, with few material needs—discouraging prospects for merchants or missionaries in those days.

After the long, relatively peaceful and prosperous reign of Souligna Vongsa, Laos fell on evil days. With no son to succeed him (the stern king had put his only son to death for having seduced the wife of a high court official) power was briefly wielded by the highest-ranking mandarin, Tien Thala, who was in turn overthrown by a provincial governor. Family dissensions among Souligna Vongsa's descendants eventually led, in 1707, to one of his nephews, Sai Ong Hué setting himself up as a prince in Vientiane and a grandson, Kitsarat, in Luang Prabang which he declared an independent kingdom.

This was the beginning of the breakup of the state as

*Arthur J. Dommen, *Conflict in Laos: The Politics of Neutralization,* Praeger, New York, 1964.

founded by Fa Ngoun and the opening up of Laos to partition by foreign invaders. Six years later further dissension resulted in another kingdom being set up at Champassac in the South, where a number of provinces seceded from Sai Ong Hué's Vientiane kingdom. Thus by 1713 there were three kingdoms, Luang Prabang in the North, Vientiane in the Center and Champassac in the South. But unity or cohesion did not exist even within the three kingdoms themselves, local feudal rulers declaring themselves independent of the royal capitals, and another kingdom was set up in Xieng Khouang. Bitter wars between the kingdoms laid the country open again to invasions from traditional enemies in Siam, Burma and Annam.

By 1778, the Vientiane kingdom had become a tributary state of Siam. After an unsuccessful uprising by the vassalized Chao (Prince) Anou in 1825, the kingdom of Vientiane was annexed by Siam.* A few years later (1832) Annam took over the neighboring kingdom of Xieng Khouang. By this time Siam had also annexed the Champassac kingdom and all that was left of the Laos of the Fa Ngoun-Sam Sen Thai dynasty was Luang Prabang which Annam claimed as a vassal state but which in fact was paying tribute to Siam.

This was still the situation in 1862 when French colonialism began in Indochina with the occupation of the western provinces of Cochin-China, the southernmost part of Vietnam. The following year the French pushed into Cambodia from their bases in Cochin-China and then steadily extended their occupation to central (Annam) and northern (Tonking) Vietnam, leaving Laos until Vietnam and Cambodia had been digested.

---

*One of the results of Prince Anou's defeat was to have long-term results in Thailand. Tens of thousands of Laotians were deported by force from the Laotian side of the Mekong to the Korat Plateau on the Siamese side of the river. Their descendants today, strongly influenced by the Pathet Lao, are a major source of worry for the Thai government, forming as they do a majority of the population in Thailand's troubled northeastern provinces. There are in fact more Laotians in Thailand than in Laos.

During the period when part of Laos was a vassal of Annam and another part a vassal of Siam, there was agreement among the rulers for a type of division of the country for political, fiscal and conscription purposes, probably unique in history. Plains-dwellers whose houses were on piles would be considered Laotians with taxation and conscription loyalties to the local rulers; those with houses on ordinary ground foundations were Vietnamese with the same obligations to Annam.

Another, more classic, division of the country took place when rival western powers appeared on the scene at the end of the 19th century. The British, based in India, were expanding east into Burma and Siam, their main goal South China. The French, based on Cochin-China, having swallowed up Annam, Tonking and Cambodia, also had an eye on South China. Laos was a secondary prize on which neither side wanted to waste powder and shot.

The first showdown over Laos did not take place until 1885 when Siam, impressed by the setting up of French military outposts along the Annamite Chain overlooking Laos, launched an expedition to seize the Plain of Jars (even in those days considered a highly strategic area) and dispatched officials to Luang Prabang to tighten Siam's control over that tributary state. The French warned Bangkok that the kingdoms of Xieng Khouang and Luang Prabang were both under the sovereignty of the Court of Hué, capital of the Annam empire, now under French "protection." The upshot was that the following year France was able to appoint August Pavie, who proved to be one of the shrewdest empire-builders France has produced, as vice-consul in Luang Prabang. Pavie thus started the long process of intrigue and demonstrations of force by which France gradually positioned itself for the complete take-over of Laos.

By using the Treaty of Protectorate under which the empire of Annam had been absorbed, Pavie managed to extend French influence to any regions which, even in the flimsiest fashion, had been tributaries to Annam. The final showdown came in the classic manner with the dispatch of a French naval contingent to Bangkok and a shotgun treaty was imposed on Siam, October 3, 1893, under which Siam ceded all of Laos east of the Mekong to France, that on the west bank remaining with Siam. Laos was thus neatly carved up between Britain and France as a sphere of influence, France accepting Siam's role as a British-dominated buffer state between the main bases of French and British imperialism on the Asian mainland.

In subsequent conventions, certain regions on the west bank were also transferred to France which established Vientiane as the administrative capital of its latest colony. A royal capital was maintained in Luang Prabang, with King Sisavang Vong on the throne, nominated for the post by the French Senior Resident.

Their warships in Bangkok harbor, the French were able to arrange things fairly smoothly with the rulers of Siam, but it was different with the Laotian people, especially when the French-appointed tax collectors and their agents set to work.

The first large-scale insurrection broke out in 1901, eight years after the Treaty of Bangkok was signed. It was confined to the Savannakhet and Champassac areas in the South and was led by Phocodouot, a district chief of the plains-dwelling Lao Lum. It was put down after two years, conditions in the plains not favoring partisan-type warfare. Far more successful was an uprising of the Lao Theung which comprise some 40 tribal groupings including the Kha (slaves), the poorest and most oppressed of all the Lao peoples. The Lao Theung are specially strong in the Bolovens Plateau in southern Laos. The first leader of the revolt was Ong Keo, chief of the Lavel, the largest single tribal grouping among the Lao Theung. After Ong Keo was killed by treachery—a local French Resident under the pretext of peace negotiations having arranged a private meeting at which he shot the Lavel chief with his pistol—leadership passed to one of the great Laotians of his day, Komadome, also from the Lao Theung.

Despite tremendous difficulties of communication, Komadome weaved together a resistance movement covering many provinces, with a political program which paved the way for alliances with other tribal groupings and even the Lao Lum in some areas. He developed a written language for the Lao Theung people and came closest to being the first real national leader since the days of Fa Ngoun, the difference being that his strength was based on popular support and not on subjugating rival princes.

The French mobilized at one time the major part of their forces in Indochina against Komadome, using everything from elephants to fighter planes to crush the movement. Starting in 1910, it lasted until 1937 before being finally crushed after a two years' blockade of Komadome's main base area at Phu Luong near the Vietnamese frontier. One of the resistance leader's sons, Khampan, later told me how the end came:

"In the final phase, the French bombed us from the air and moved up with three battalions of troops, 200 elephants, horse-borne troops and Alsatian dogs to track us down. My father and my eldest brother Si Thone laid an ambush for their advance party, but the French were shown another track by a traitor and surprised our headquarters from behind. We rushed out at the noise of dogs but my father had forgotten his pistol. As he ran to get it, he was shot in the back. The elephants were used to trample down our houses and the people inside them. Si Thone was wounded and taken prisoner with another brother. Three younger brothers were thrown into a ravine and three still smaller ones were shot or died later of starvation. The elephants were used to charge into the villages and any of our people who survived were shot or bayoneted."

Khamphan managed to escape capture for another eight months but finally was caught and sentenced to 20 years in prison, Si Thone to life imprisonment. Released by the Pathet Lao uprising in August 1945, Khamphan and Si Thone immediately joined the resistance movement and are today high-ranking leaders of the Pathet Lao forces in southern Laos. Komadome remains a legendary figure whose exploits have entered into the country's folk lore.

There were numerous other uprisings during the first phase

of French occupation, but nothing compared to Komadome's 27-years' war. The various movements were uncoordinated, organized on local or regional scales, and the French could concentrate their forces to crush them. This phase of resistance against the French ended with World War II and the temporary occupation of Laos by the Japanese.

When Vichy France capitulated to the Japanese invaders of Indochina in December 1941, a new stage of the Laotian independence struggle was ushered in. For the first time it was to be organized on a national basis, uniting all tribes and races, the mountain people and the plains-dwellers, eventually engulfing the cities as well. In the struggle against the French attempt at recolonization after the defeat of Japan, an effective unity was forged among the peoples of Indochina who were able to wrest independence from France, which had been supported in the first Indochina war by the U.S.

When U.S. imperialism tried to fill what its leaders considered a "power vacuum" caused by the forced departure of the French, it was confronted with the fierce resistance of the Laotian people. Their leaders understood what was happening, despite the teleguided form in which the new attempt at colonization at first took on—the manipulation of local placemen, a long list of Laotian equivalents of Ngo Dinh Diem and other "strong men" who temporarily served U.S. interests in South Vietnam. The long struggle against French colonialism had aroused the political consciousness of the Laotian people to the point at which they could recognize the signs of attempted domination. The Lao Lum peasants and the Lao Theung and Lao Xung tribespeople did not need computers to sense the aims of U.S. intervention any more than does a hare when he hears the barking of hounds on his tracks. And they were able to distinguish between leaders ready to sell out their independence and those ready to accept any sacrifices to defend it.

In terms of population, economic and social development or natural resources, mid-20th century Laos hardly seemed qualified for a leading role on the stage of history. Unfortunately for the leisurely, gentle Laotian people, steeped in Buddhist tolerance and pacifism, their country was forced into playing just such an unrewarding role. Through no fault or desire of its own, Laos became a domino of the Pentagon-CIA whizz-kids, the toppling of which could be presented as a major defeat and disaster for the "free world" and thus a *"causa belli."*

2

Background to Hidden War

Just as the role of the United States in South Vietnam only gradually impinged upon public awareness, its role in a hidden war in Laos* is now also gradually emerging from the shadows of official secrecy. U.S. mythologists, when smoked out into the open by facts or incidents too blatant to escape public notice, pretend that U.S. involvement is something new, made necessary by a "Ho Chi Minh trail" to South Vietnam or by North Vietnamese "aggression" against Laos.

The presence or otherwise of "Ho Chi Minh trails" or North Vietnamese troops are of incidental importance only. They have nothing to do with the origins, aims and extent of U.S. intervention. This has long ago been escalated into "special war" in Laos on a scale proportionately greater than in South Vietnam in March 1965 when "special war" was escalated into "limited war" with the commitment of U.S. combat divisions.

What is happening in Laos today is a logical step-by-step development of processes set in motion nearly 20 years ago, as part of Washington's global crusading policies of the time. If the situation has not yet escalated into "limited war"—and if the latter is in fact averted—this will not be due to some ideological change of heart in Washington but to the bitter lessons inflicted on U.S. strategists by the armed forces of the Vietnamese and Laotian national liberation movements.

*In *The Furtive War: The United States in Vietnam and Laos* (International Publishers, New York, 1963) the author drew attention to the extent of America's secret war in South Vietnam and the beginning of a similar one in Laos.

There were also other factors which Washington might well have heeded. By the end of 1969, China, emerging from the self-imposed isolation of the "cultural revolution," began showing an interest again in what was happening in the perimeter areas. More specifically, the Soviet Union on November 3, in the form of a note sent by Foreign Minister Andrei Gromyko to participants in the 1962 Geneva Conference on Laos, registered a sharp protest against U.S. intervention in Laos. The note expressed "serious concern" at the "alarming situation that has been created in Laos as a result of the further widening scale of U.S. interference in the internal affairs of that country, specifically the participation of its armed forces in military actions on Laotian territory." The declaration went on to say that the Soviet government "condemns U.S. actions in Laos and stresses that all responsibility for the dangerous situation taking place there rests with those forces which are moving actually to open a new front in the war of aggression against the peoples of Southeast Asia." Despite such warning and the lessons that should have been learned from the successful resistance of the liberation forces in Vietnam and Laos, the military establishment of which President Nixon seems to be a willing prisoner continued on its course toward further expansion of the war.

As another decade came to an end and the 1970's loomed over the horizon, Laos, in the eyes of President Nixon's Southeast Asia experts, seemed to be shaping up satisfactorily for almost the first time since the United States became interested in that corner of Asia. Unlimited dollars and tonnage of bombs, napalm, forest- and crop-killing chemicals; thousands of U.S. "advisers"; highly-paid treachery in Vientiane, and "special forces" on the battlefield had produced results. Maps would show a large part of the rural population where the Pentagon wanted them—and the CIA had put them—behind barbed wire. Between the highly concentrated "population clusters," as they were officially called, would be shown "white areas" where no one lives, nothing grows, emptied if not of the Pathet Lao fish, at least of the sea in which they swam.

Above all, the highly strategic Plain of Jars* was now in the hands of the "free world" and a 24-hour shuttle service of CIA planes was flying in men and materials to transform it into the network of bases that for so long had been the dream of Pentagon "hawks."

For the first time in eight years, the Plain of Jars was in the hands of the U.S.-backed rightist forces, which also for the first time had won a notable victory, although it proved short-lived. But because it was a victory, President Nixon could not resist referring to the U.S. role in the affair, which did not pass unnoticed in the United States. Newspapers began to show an interest in the extent of U.S. ivolvement, prodding Congress to show an interest also. Hence the Senate inquiry in the Fall of 1969, preceded by an on-the-spot investigation by *New York Times* correspondent Henry Kamm. The preliminary results produced scandalized astonishment at what had been going on over the years behind the backs of the American public.

"What strikes me most," said Senator Fulbright† "is that an operation of this size could be carried out without members of the Senate knowing it—and without the public knowing! U.S. involvement in the war on such a large scope," he continued, "presents a dilemma of major proportions. I knew we were doing a little of this and a little of that in Laos, but I had no idea it was a major operation of this kind." Referring specifically to only one secret CIA-Pentagon operation, the shuttling of an army of tribal mercenaries between a base in Thailand and across the border in Laos, he revealed that at least $150 million a year was being spent "to supply, arm, train and transport a clandestine army of 36,000 men . . . This force which we supply and train . . . is backed

---

*The Plain gets its name from huge grey jars, three to eight feet in height, ranged in strips up to a mile long and several jars wide. Their origin is still a mystery and they have now been bombed to bits as the U.S. Air Force contribution to creating archeological ruins!

†In an interview with Murray Marder, published in the Washington *Post*, October 30, 1969, after preliminary hearings before a Senate Foreign Relations sub-committee under Senator Stuart Symington.

up by an enormous air force. I don't mean just helicopters; I mean the U.S. Air Force operating out of Thailand." And to emphasize how serious he considered the situation, he continued: "This is not in my view an undertaking by the CIA as such. The CIA is operating under orders of the National Security Council, and a committee which is appointed by the Council, which is directly responsible to the President." He added that not only the Nixon administration, but also the Kennedy and Johnson had been involved in the secret Laos intervention.

Senator Stuart Symington, on the eve of the sub-committee hearings, charged the administration with deliberately keeping secret from the public the fact that Americans were involved in a war in Laos. As reported by UPI (October 19, 1969), "He called the situation a 'travesty' and charged that 'high' government officials have wrapped activities there in a cloak of 'secrecy'." Some of them continued to do so by refusing to testify before Symington's sub-committee. President Nixon himself carried the policy of secrecy still further by refusing to permit the full publication of the evidence the sub-committee was able to obtain. Only a heavily censored transcript was made available to the public.

Eventually, under strong congressional and public pressure and six months after the sub-committee had completed its work, 237 pages of the censored part of the transcript were released "after more than 100 meetings with State Department and other officials," wrote Murray Marder in the Washington *Post* (April 20, 1970). The revelations contained therein made it clear why Nixon was so coy about disclosing what he and his predecessors had been up to in Laos and why another ten per cent of the transcript was still under censorship wraps. The report confirmed that the United States had indeed been engaged in air operations in Laos since 1964 at a cost of 'billions of dollars' and over 200 American lives." The transcript revealed that the U.S. ambassador to Laos between 1964 and 1969, William H. Sullivan, was in fact the commander-in-chief of extensive military operations inside the country.

"The new record shows that the war in Laos involved far more than the '1,040 Americans . . . stationed in Laos' that the President's guarded statement listed. That is only the tip of the iceberg. The hearings disclosed, as sub-committee sources put it, that 'tens of thousands' of Americans are engaged in the Laotian war."

Murray Marder's report goes on to say that "Censorship took out of the transcript all summary figures on costs; every reference to the Central Intelligence Agency's operations, which include training, equipping, supplying and directing the 'clandestine' army of up to 36,000 Meo tribesmen in Laos commanded by Gen. Vang Pao; all references to the use of Thailand's forces in Laos; details of U.S. air operations from Laos; figures showing the escalation of American air strikes in Laos during bombing 'pauses' or in the halt in the air war against North Vietnam and other critical facts."

As a result of the public alarm over deeper American involvement in Laos (even as President Nixon was promising to withdraw from Vietnam), the U.S. Senate on December 15, 1969 adopted a resolution, in connection with a defense appropriations bill, intended according to its sponsors to end the danger of U.S. armed intervention in Laos and Thailand. The effort received wide support, but it soon became clear, with the publication of the text, that unfortunately the resolution included no ban against the kind of "special war" in Laos over which the recent revelations had aroused wide indignation. The key phrase states: "None of the funds appropriated by this act shall be used to finance the introduction of American ground troops into Laos or Thailand."

The Air Force, helicopter units, Green Berets, artillery, communications and other support facilities—all the paraphernalia of "special war"—remain immune. Not a dollar would be cut from the budget which finances such activities. At most, the resolution seeks to prevent immediate escalation into "limited war"; but it suits the Nixon version of "Asians fighting Asians" with American help. Small wonder that President Nixon could tell Senate leaders the resolution was "definitely in line with Administration policy," and that the White House press secretary could commend it as an "endorsement" rather than a curbing of that policy. In fact, it turned out that the resolution had been sent to the President for approval and then had been passed at a secret session of the Senate with reporters excluded from the galleries.

One aspect of the recent revelations that cannot escape general notice is the secrecy, skulduggery and outright lying at the highest levels which has characterized U.S. intervention in Laos from the very beginning. The public at large finally has caught a glimpse, still limited, of the really dirty work going on in areas remote from the spotlight of publicity. I have been a witness to this in Laos, off and on for the past 15 years. Professionally, I am gratified that other western journalists, especially American journalists, are finally on the scent of what has been going on. However, I think it is only fair to say that had there not been the national crisis over the failures in Vietnam and fears lest more Vietnams were developing under the surface, the spotlight would not have been turned on Laos.

Where did it all start?

It was in the year 1949 that the Chinese Red Army was tearing the guts out of what was left of Chiang Kai-shek's U.S.-backed Kuomintang forces, pushing them back in great encircling actions south of the Yangtse river, grinding them to pieces and sweeping what was left of them off the Chinese mainland to Hainan island. (From where those who survived another shattering defeat were later removed by U.S. planes and warships to the comparative safety of Taiwan.) It was the year in which the Chinese People's Republic was proclaimed in Peking. It was also the year in which General "Wild Bill" Donovan, who had headed America's war-time Office of Strategic Services and later fathered the CIA which succeeded it, sent one of his right-hand men, Major James Thompson into Laos to set up an espionage network there, linked with another being set up across the border in northeast Thailand.

(Donovan, an enthusiastic specialist in espionage in Southeast Asia, was later appointed U.S. ambassador to Thailand to run things on the spot.)

Even a cursory glance at the map of Laos explains its fascination for the "hawks" of those days, whose major preoccupation was how to put Chiang Kai-shek back onto the Chinese mainland. How best to support the remnant Kuomintang troops still being mopped up in Southwest China? How to make the best use of the considerable Kuomintang force under General Li Mi which had escaped into Burma to be immediately taken over by Donovan and his staff? Later, after Vo Nguyen Giap's troops had won a decisive victory over French forces along Vietnam's northern frontiers and opened up communications between the Vietminh-controlled areas and People's China, the question of halting the onward march of the Vietnam revolution was also on the agenda.

Thus, Laos became important strategically. It has frontiers with Thailand, Burma, China, Cambodia and Vietnam—and once the latter had been divided at the 17th parallel by the 1954 Geneva Agreements, Laos had frontiers with *both* North and South Vietnam. Furthermore, this meant common boundaries with two socialist states, People's China and the Democratic Republic of Vietnam, and with the neutral states of Cambodia and Burma. It also had the tempting strategic Plain of Jars, where enough air power could be based to dominate the whole of South China and the mainland countries of Southeast Asia. With the development of rocketry, the two serried ranges of Laotian mountains running northeast-southeast along the frontier with Vietnam, provided an irresistible appeal for the Pentagon's rocketeers.

My own first contact with the Laotian problem was in early March 1954. The Geneva Conference had already been scheduled. Apart from discussing a peaceful settlement in Korea—my main interest at the time—the Conference was also to discuss a ceasefire in Indochina. I decided to visit the Vietminh headquarters in the North Vietnamese jungle and find out what I could about the Indochina war. There, in addition to meeting President Ho Chi Minh, Pham Van Dong and other Vietnamese leaders for the first time, I also met the head of the Pathet Lao, Prince Souphanouvong. It was my first-ever meeting with a Prince and also my first realization that Indochina was not a single state, as most non-specialists regarded it in those days, but made up of the three separate entities of Vietnam, Cambodia and Laos.

Souphanouvong was at Ho Chi Minh's headquarters to coordinate policies for the forthcoming Geneva Conference where Laos was bound to be discussed. Also the battle of Dien Bien Phu was just shaping up and the Pathet Lao forces were blocking French attempts to open up a land route from their Laos bases through to the valley of Dien Bien Phu.

Souphanouvong is a compact, short but powerfully built man. His face, walnut brown after years living in the open, with its high cheekbones and broad forehead, reinforces the impression of strength, intelligence and vitality. Like most of his race, he has jet black hair and eyes. He expresses himself with vigor and in the clear, direct terms of a technician, sure of his subject, with no time lost in the superficial courtesies so often encountered in Asia, even among progressives if they have feudal backgrounds. Despite his court upbringing, Souphanouvong, as I later discovered during visits to the Pathet Lao areas, identified himself completely with his people.

Speaking an impeccable French, with clarifying remarks in very good English, Souphanouvong at our first meeting gave me a concentrated briefing on the history of the Pathet Lao and the ups and downs of the Laotian resistance struggle up to the military-political situation at that moment. Briefly it was as follows:

From the time the French occupied Laos, resistance in some form or place, mainly by the ethnic minorities, never ceased. But the various uprisings were invariably crushed. As national cohesion was non-existent, the French could exploit differences between the Lao Lum and the ethnic minorities, fomenting and exploiting inter-tribal quarrels. They could concentrate their forces to suppress the uncoordinated uprisings one at a time. The development of the resistance forces in Vietnam against the French and Japanese in the early 1940's stimulated ideas of a similar united struggle in Laos. A successful uprising had been staged in August 1945, as in Vietnam. Also as in Vietnam, the French returned in force a few months later to try and restore their colonial rule. A resistance struggle had been waged ever since in close coordination with that of the Vietminh. As for Prince Souphanouvong's own role, part of it emerged at that first meeting but mainly this was pieced together later.

Souphanouvong was the youngest of 20 sons of Prince Boun Khong who headed one of Laos' three reigning families, each with its separate capital—at Luang Prabang where Souphanouvong grew up, at Vientiane, and at Paksé in the South. Boun Khong's eldest son, Prince Phetsarat, had been the last viceroy of Laos under the French. In between the youngest and eldest sons and born of a different mother was Prince Souvanna Phouma. It was Phetsarat who brought up the two half-brothers when their father died and it was he—a progressive individual for his day—who later sent them abroad with instructions to study subjects which would be of practical use in developing their backward country. Phetsarat had set the example by graduating in mechanical engineering in Paris, with printing machinery as his specialty. The half-brothers also studied in Paris, Souvanna Phouma taking a triple degree in marine, electrical and civil engineering; Souphanouvong graduating as a road and bridge-building engineer at France's famous Ecole des Ponts et Chaussées. Both were brilliant students and at the time they graduated, and for many years to come, the three princes were the only engineers in Laos.

In 1937, at the time of the Popular Front government in France, Souphanouvong was doing post-graduate work on the docks at Bordeaux and Le Havre. Like Ho Chi Minh, he soon appreciated that the average Frenchman in France was very different from the colonialist specimens who lorded it over his compatriots in his own country. His contacts were with progressive intellectuals and the French workers. He was deeply impressed by French revolutionary and humanist culture and the contrast this offered with everything he had experienced of French colonialism. He was stimulated by the contagious, progressive spirit of the great days of Popular Front rule with its overtones of anti-colonialism.

There were no roads or bridges to be built under the French administration in Laos, so Souphanouvong started his engineering career over the border in Vietnam. He was appalled by the living and working conditions of laborers on the rubber plantations through which he built roads and in the labor camps alongside railway construction sites on which he worked. His contempt for French colonialism reached flash point when Indochina was ceded to the Japanese without the French "protectors" firing a shot in defense of the Vietnamese, Cambodian and Laotian peoples.

After his contacts with militant progressives in France, it was natural that he contacted progressives in Vietnam, many of them organized in the Indochinese Communist party. There came a fateful meeting with Ho Chi Minh. After a long exchange of opinions about colonialism in their two countries, Souphanouvong put the blunt question as to what he should do for his own people. He got an equally blunt reply: "Seize power from the colonialists!" And Ho Chi Minh went on to explain how he was preparing to do this in Vietnam. Souphanouvong set about doing the same thing, first by contacting young Laotian patriots in Vietnam, then returning to form resistance groups on Laotian soil on the pattern of those being formed by Uncle Ho for a seizure of power in Vietnam.

A successful uprising was staged in August 1945, mainly by groups of intellectuals in the cities and patriotic elements within the French-formed army, whom the very persuasive Souphanouvong had won over to his side. The weakness of the resistance forces was that they had no roots in the countryside. Souphanouvong tried to mobilize his brothers, a number of whom were leading cadres in the army. Phetsarat gave the movement his blessing from above; Souvanna

Phouma agreed to accept a post in the new government formed after the king abdicated and independence was declared.

Then the French returned. As in their original occupation of Indochina, they left the reoccupation of Laos until (thanks to British troops ostensibly sent to Vietnam to disarm and repatriate the Japanese) they had consolidated their positions in South and Central Vietnam and Cambodia and had secured their lines of communication in those areas. When they were ready, they made a three-pronged invasion of Laos, up from Cambodia, across from Central Vietnam, down from Kuomintang China. The Pathet Lao forces fought bravely but were defeated in a decisive battle on March 21, 1946 at Thakhek on the Mekong, a strategic junction where the main road leading west from Vietnam meets the main road leading north from Cambodia. The French made full use of their monopoly of air power and artillery. Souphanouvong personally commanded the Pathet Lao troops and was seriously wounded, carried by the remnants of his forces over the frontier into Thailand. It took another five months for the French to consolidate their positions in the main towns and the roads leading to them.

A Laotian government-in-exile was set up in Bangkok, the government of Thailand at that time favoring the independence movements in Vietnam and Laos. Prince Phetsarat was Head of State and other key members included princes Souphanouvong and Souvanna Phouma and a certain Katay Don Sasorith of part Vietnamese origin who had joined the former resistance government in August 1945, once power had been seized.

After recovering from his wounds, Souphanouvong began to analyze the reasons for the military defeat and concluded that the main mistake had been in basing the resistance exclusively on the towns and on trying to fight the French on their terms. He and a handful of supporters started to study the revolutionary experiences of the ethnic minorities and the Lao Lum peasants and concluded that the peasantry and tribespeople in the mountains and jungle provided precious reserves for a long resistance struggle, which must be based not only on the urban intelligentsia but above all on the peasantry and ethnic minorities. A sense of unity and nationhood must be forged. He tried to persuade other members of the government-in-exile to support him in a new start, based on mobilizing the whole Laotian people in armed struggle. But when it came to the point of leaving the comfortable life of exiles in Bangkok, the others decided to adopt a wait and see attitude. Souphanouvong returned alone in 1947 to organize a resistance movement. He found that the remnants of his original and widely separated armed forces had been continuing as well as they could on their own. Loosely coordinated commands had been set up in the mountains along the frontiers with Vietnam. Some of the tribespeople had started their own resistance movements. It was a situation in search of a leader. Souphanouvong accepted the role.

The French in the meantime had restored the king to nominal power, which did not in fact extend beyond the palace grounds, and had experimented with a number of short-lived puppet governments. But no one with any prestige was prepared to serve. Eventually the French turned to the government-in-exile in Thailand. The first to desert, slinking away without even a word to his colleagues, was Katay. (He was later to catch the eye of John Foster Dulles with a book, *Laos: Ideal Cornerstone in the Anti-Communist Struggle in Southeast Asia*—sure bait for Dulles' talent scouts!) Souvanna Phouma was the next to desert and was used by the French to persuade the others. Only Phetsarat, too old to join Souphanouvong in the jungle, refused to return to serve the French. He remained in exile when Souvanna Phouma, in 1949, led the rest of the former provisional government back to serve in a puppet administration in Vientiane.

Souphanouvong in the meantime had succeeded in welding the various patriotic elements among the three main racial groupings into a single national unit which was given concrete form at a nationwide congress in mid-August 1950. Delegates from all racial groupings and the most important sub-groups, from all social strata and the Buddhist clergy came together from many parts of the country and elected a resistance government, headed by Prince Souphanouvong. The conference also elected a central committee of the Neo Lao Itsala,* the political expression of the Pathet Lao armed forces in whose name the struggle had been waged till then. By that time resistance bases had been consolidated in virtually every province of upper, central and lower Laos.

The following year, national unity was expanded into solidarity among the whole Indochinese people with the formation of an alliance between the Neo Lao Itsala and corresponding bodies in Vietnam and Cambodia.† This was an historic event, as it brought the three peoples together in organizational form for the first time. Until then it was the French who had the monopoly of using the entire territory of Indochina as a single military entity, moving their troops through the territory of one country to outflank resistance forces in a neighboring one, just as Cambodian and Vietnamese territory had been used as bases for the original subjugation of Laos. From 1951 onward, Vietnamese and Laotian resistance forces fought side by side, using each other's territory to outflank the French and to coordinate their military activities.

Starting in 1950, the United States directly subsidized French efforts to wipe out the resistance forces, to the extent of 25 million dollars a year, but the Pathet Lao units continued to grow in strength and influence.

The culminating point in the war itself and in the cooperation between the Vietminh and Pathet Lao forces was shaping up at the time of my first meeting with Souphanouvong; the cream of the French Expeditionary Corps was

---

*The Neo Lao Itsala (Laotian Freedom Front) was later broadened into the Neo Lao Haksat (Laotian Patriotic Front). Pathet Lao means Land of the Lao.

† The Lien Viet (Vietnam National United Front), formed in 1951 to succeed the Vietminh (Vietnam Independence League), and the Nekhum Issarak Khmer (Cambodian Freedom Front).

bottled up and encircled by Giap's forces at Dien Bien Phu, just across the border from Laos in northwest Vietnam, and all routes of access and exit were solidly blocked by Pathet Lao veterans.

By that time, the United States was footing 80 per cent of the costs of France's "dirty war" in Indochina and plans were being made to intervene directly with U.S. combat troops, not to mention U.S. air power.

3

Getting in Deeper

When it became obvious that neither dollars, nor the U.S. tanks, planes and artillery, the remnants of which still litter the valley of Dien Bien Phu, could save the French from military defeat the Pentagon proposed direct military intervention. This proposal was made after agreement had already been reached among the Big Powers to discuss a ceasefire at Geneva! Former U.S. Assistant Secretary of State for Far Eastern Affairs, Roger Hilsman, described the plan as follows:*

"By mid-March (1954), the French defenders at Dien Bien Phu were in trouble and Washington was worried. Admiral Radford, Chairman of the American Joint Chiefs of Staff, proposed to the French High Command that sixty American bombers from Clark Field in the Philippines escorted by 150 Navy fighters from the Seventh Fleet should conduct a raid on the forces ringing Dienbienphu in an attempt to 'eliminate' Viet Minh artillery installations and communications— 'Operation Vulture' it was named."

Congressional leaders were briefed. Skeptical (after the Korean experience where "Operation Strangler" had failed against the Korean-Chinese transport system) of Radford's promise that "one strike would do the job—but that if not, surely a second would," according to Hilsman they laid down three conditions that would have to be met before they sanctioned the plan. These represent a striking illustration of the congressional leaders' devotion to the independence and

*Roger Hilsman, *To Move A Nation*, pp. 100-01. Hereafter, all references to Hilsman are to this book, with page numbers given in text.

111

self-determination of nations! The conditions were that "support to the French be multilateral," the French "should speed up the process of granting Indochina its independence," and "should agree not to withdraw their military forces from Indochina." How the third condition could be reconciled with the second, Hilsman does not explain.

Dulles promptly set to work on Anthony Eden, the British Foreign Secretary, to try and provide the first offer of "multilateral support." Eden describes in his book, *Full Circle (1960)*, his own and Churchill's indignation when they saw that Dulles was trying to push them into the position of not only getting involved in, but seeming to be the instigators of, "multilateral support"—that is, a Korean War-type international intervention.

While Dulles was doing his best, the Pentagon went ahead with even more ambitious planning. General Matthew B. Ridgway, then Army Chief of Staff and, after his experiences as "UN" Commander in Korea, a disbeliever in the decisive role of air power, sent a team of specialists to estimate how many U.S. combat troops would be necessary to make intervention effective. They reported back, still according to Hilsman who had access to all the documents, "that at least five divisions would be needed at the outset, rising to ten or more as the fighting progressed." Ridgway was against the project and in his book, *The Korean War (1967)* he later commented that his specialists' report "played a considerable, perhaps decisive part in persuading our Government not to embark on that tragic adventure."

Although Radford's plan was aimed specifically at rescuing the French at Dien Bien Phu, it would certainly have involved Laos as well as Vietnam since Pentagon thinking was in terms of the war in Indochina and not in its component parts. In the French winter-spring offensive of 1953-54, Thailand-based planes flown by U.S. pilots had caused heavy human and material losses in raids on the Pathet Lao controlled areas of North Laos, according to official Pathet Lao documents.

Dulles turned up for the early stages of the Geneva Conference and tried desperately to persuade those countries that had taken part in the Korean War (whose foreign ministers were in Geneva for the Korean part of the conference) to join in a new war of intervention in Indochina. But troops were offered only by South Korea and Australia, with Thailand and the Philippines making half-hearted offers "in principle." When Churchill finally and emphatically killed the plan by refusing British support and Canada's Lester Pearson did the same, Dulles left Geneva in a rage. Those of us who were there will never forget his expression as he stalked out of the former League of Nations building, obviously boiling with fury after receiving the decisive telegram on Churchill's refusal. He left Geneva within hours but continued from Washington to do everything possible to avert a ceasefire, even offering French Foreign Minister Bidault a couple of A-bombs if that would keep France in the war. But the Laniel-Bidault government fell, to be replaced by Pierre Mendes-France who set himself the deadline of July 20 by which to get a ceasefire or resign.

Dulles still had a few more tricks to play. In a dramatic and little-publicized meeting with Eden and Mendes-France in Paris on July 13, one week before the latter had pledged to have a "ceasefire or bust," Dulles laid his plan for SEATO on the table, demanding that it be set up immediately as the instrument for emergency intervention in Indochina. After a stormy session during which both Dulles and Mendes-France pounded the table with their fists, the French Premier, staunchly supported by Eden, rejected the "emergency intervention" but accepted the SEATO concept, on condition that it be set up only after all possibilities of arranging a ceasefire had been exhausted. Dulles stormed away from that meeting in as black a rage as at the time of his earlier setback in Geneva. But there were still one or two more cards to play.

In her efforts to break the fighting solidarity of the Indochinese peoples and, according to how hard-pressed she was on the battlefield—or by her allies—France handed out bits and pieces of independence to Cambodia and Laos, but in such a form that whatever was given could easily be taken back if she could win the upper hand. By the time the Geneva Conference on Indochina got under way, Souvanna Phouma was nominally prime minister of an "independent" Laos, represented at Geneva by Defense Minister Kou Voravong and Foreign Minister Phoui Sananikone, member of an old feudal family who had long cooperated with the French. The trappings of "independence" had been hastily fashioned to keep Souphanouvong's resistance government away from the conference table.

As the clock ticked away toward midnight on the fateful night of July 20, agreement on ceasefire procedures having been reached between the French and Vietminh delegations, it became known that insuperable difficulties had arisen within the Laotian delegation. Sananikone refused to sign on the pretext that it implied recognition of the Pathet Lao because of the provisions for regrouping their forces in the two northern provinces of Phong Saly and Sam Neua. (The final agreements were not signed until dawn on July 21 because the Cambodian delegation refused to agree to a similar regrouping procedure for the Khmer Issarak forces which were proportionately much smaller than those of the Pathet Lao.) During that night of July 20, the "hawks" among the American journalists confidently were predicting that the deadline would never be met, that Mendes-France would have to resign and the Geneva Conference would collapse.* They were counting above all on the Laotian delegation. But in the end Kou Voravong signed for Laos and the Geneva Conference came to a successful end as far as negotiating a ceasefire was concerned.

Back in Vientiane, Kou Voravong revealed in the National Assembly that an agent of the United States had paid one million dollars into a Swiss bank account for Sananikone in

---

*To re-read Joe Alsop's reports of the final stages of the Geneva Conference is to get an idea of the inspired pessimism at the time.

return for his pledge that the Laotian delegation would not sign the Geneva Agreements. A few days later, Kou Voravaong was assassinated as he sat—a dinner guest—with his back to the window in the home of Phoui Sananikone. The assassin, who fired through the window, stepped into a waiting boat and crossed the Mekong river into Thailand.

In addition to his "crimes" of having signed the Geneva Agreements (on instructions from Prime Minister Souvanna Phouma) and of having revealed Phoui Sananikone's role at Geneva, nine days earlier Kou Voravong had arranged, and participated in, the first meeting between Souvanna Phouma and Souphanouvong. This represented a start in the political negotiations provided for under the Geneva Agreements to bring about national reconciliation between the royal government and the Pathet Lao. To cap everything, Kou Voravong had also revealed and denounced in the National Assembly plans to stage a treacherous attack on the Pathet Lao forces as they withdrew from their bases and regrouped in accordance with the Geneva Agreements. A friend of the assassinated minister later told me that he had accepted an invitation from Phoui Sananikone to "talk things over" but that Kou Voravong had gone to the dinner determined not to yield an inch. The assassin's bullet in his back was the result.

At Geneva, Bidault, who during a United Nations debate had once referred to Ho Chi Minh as a "non-existent phantom," had tried to pretend that Souphanouvong and the Pathet Lao were also "non-existent phantoms" and that the only question to be discussed was the withdrawal of "Vietminh aggressors" from Laos. However, when it came to discussing ceasefire details over maps, the French had to recognize officially what their field commanders knew very well, namely, that the Pathet Lao forces held important bases and liberated areas throughout the whole of Laos. It was the French who insisted that in order to make a ceasefire and separation of combatant forces effective, the Pathet Lao were to withdraw from the ten central and southern provinces and regroup in Phong Saly and Sam Neua, the two northeastern provinces having common frontiers with Vietnam and China respectively.* It was a blow to have to abandon their old bases, especially solid resistance areas in Attopeu and Saravane provinces and the Bolovens Plateau. But as the counterpart to the regrouping was to be nationwide elections which the Pathet Lao was sure to win, it seemed but a temporary sacrifice. Sam Neua and Phong Saly were, however, provinces in which the Pathet Lao was relatively weak at the time of regrouping.

The political upheaval which followed the assassination of Kou Voravong and its implications ended in Souvanna Phouma resigning as prime minister to be replaced by Katay. The latter, who faithfully served the French in the office of Senior Resident, then jumped on the bandwagon of the first resistance government and deserted to the French again in Bangkok, now emerged as Washington's No. 1 choice as a Laotian Ngo Dinh Diem. Katay's wife by second marriage was the sister of Prince Boun Oum of Champassac whom Katay, with U.S. support, was grooming to replace the ailing King Sissavang Vong on the throne at Luang Prabang. With Katay in power in Vientiane and unlimited dollars at his disposal, Dulles was ready to enter upon a more active phase of upsetting the Geneva Agreements, with the United States moving into the "power vacuum" which would be caused in Laos by the French departure.

A fascinating account of the real plot hatched between Dulles, the CIA and the U.S. Joint Chiefs of Staff is given by Brig. General James M. Gavin who, in the period of which he was writing, was Ridgway's Deputy Chief of Army Staff, in

---

*As an example of how those in high places are ill-informed one could cite ex-President Kennedy's special adviser Arthur Schlesinger, Jr. In *A Thousand Days: John F. Kennedy in the White House* (Houghton Mifflin, Boston, 1965) he writes: "In 1953, the Pathet Lao with Vietminh support occupied two provinces in northeastern Laos" (p. 324). In fact it was in late 1954, without Vietminh support, and under the specific provisions of the Geneva Agreements.

charge of plans.* As the French had "unwisely folded" and were "acting in their own self-interest rather than in the interests of the free world as a whole," writes Gavin, it was up to the United States "to assume the full burden of combat against Communism in that area." Immediately after the Geneva Conference, the Joint Chiefs of Staff "began with the highest priority to study a proposal to send combat troops into the Red River delta of North Vietnam." Ridgway, as during the Dien Bien Phu crisis, was wary. He sent Gavin to South Vietnam to size up what sort of forces would be needed. Gavin and his experts agreed such an operation would probably mean war with China, as the U.S. Navy wanted to occupy Hainan Island, being "unwilling to risk their ships in the Haiphong area without first invading and capturing the island." As the Chinese might react by reopening the Korean front, the Joint Chiefs must make "the agonizing decision as to whether we should wait to be attacked in Korea, or whether we should take the initiative in reopening that front."

To occupy the Red River delta and capture Haiphong and Hanoi, Gavin estimated, would take "eight combat divisions supported by thirty-five engineer battalions and all the artillery and logistical support such mammoth undertakings require."

Admiral Radford was enthusiastic for this plan, so was Dulles and the CIA. Radford was "fully supported by the Chief of Staff of the Air Force and the Chief of Naval Operations." Gavin was against it because of the Army horror of getting bogged down in a land war in Asia and tangling with the Chinese again. Ridgway agreed with Gavin and went over Radford's head to persuade Eisenhower to veto the scheme. Instead it was decided to build up Ngo Dinh Diem's army in South Vietnam to do the job in a famous "March to the North." The Radford-Dulles-CIA plan called for an invasion well before July 1956, when the elections to unify

*James M. Gavin, *Crisis Now*, Random House, New York, 1968, pp. 45-49.

Vietnam were to be held in accordance with the Geneva Agreements.

As for Laos, in February 1955, after a SEATO meeting in Bangkok, Dulles dropped in at Vientiane for a chat with Katay. The political talks arranged by Kou Voravong had finally started on December 30, 1954. While Katay played for time over procedural matters, U.S. transport planes dropped commando units into Sam Neua and Phong Saly in an attempt to wipe out the Pathet Lao bases and headquarters there. When the talks did get started, Katay's delegate produced a plan to set up a "Surrender Committee" to arrange for the disarming and surrender of the Pathet Lao forces. Obviously the Pathet Lao refused and proposed setting up a political committee to arrange the implementation of the Geneva Agreements, nationwide elections, unification of the country, integration of the Pathet Lao into the national community and other points included in the ceasefire agreement.

The talks quickly bogged down as Katay intended. It was obvious that he was playing for time and awaiting instructions which were brought personally by Dulles. A couple of weeks after the latter's visit, Katay's troops launched a major attack into Sam Neua, the beginning of a long and unsuccessful campaign to occupy that province and Phong Saly province, wipe out the Pathet Lao and present the United States with an aggressor's dream in the shape of the vast plateaus and plains of Laos from which U.S. air power could dominate the entire region. "If Laos was not precisely a dagger pointed at the heart of Kansas, it was very plainly a gateway to Southeast Asia," writes Arthur Schlesinger. The United States was in. Arms, dollars and transport planes for a start; then military "instructors," followed by "advisers" who gradually assumed tactical command of military operations. Schlesinger has some pungent comments on the early years of the Dulles plan to transform Laos into a "bulwark against Communism" and a "bastion of freedom" (policies continued by Dean Rusk and the Nixon Administration):

"In pursuit of this dream, the United States flooded the wild and primitive land with nearly $300 million by the end of 1960. This amounted to $150 for every inhabitant—more aid per capita than any other country and almost double the previous per capita income of the Laotians. Eighty-five percent of this went to pay the total bill for the Royal Laotian army, which by 1959 was outfitted in American style with jeeps, trucks and a Transportation Corps (all despite the fact that Laos had no all-weather roads) as well as Ordnance Corps, a Quartermaster Corps and Military Police. When trained at all, and effective training did not begin until 1959, the Laotian troops learned, not counter-guerrilla warfare but conventional maneuvers. Of the $300 million only $7 million went for technical cooperation and economic development."*

My own first visit to Vientiane was in May 1956. Instead of the ten days' visa I had requested, the hospitable airport officials insisted on giving me one for 21 days. A few hours after my arrival, a policeman called at my hotel saying he needed my travel document for a small change in the wording of the visa. When he returned it one word had been added: Cancelled! An embarrassed police officer said I must leave immediately. Three diplomatic missions, in separate demarchés, had demanded my expulsion. The U.S. Embassy had applied direct pressure through American "advisers" at police headquarters and the Laotian police had acted without reference to their own government. I was to be the victim of a particularly nasty short circuit of administrative procedures.

Why all this bother? The Americans and their closest allies knew that a few months previously I had seen Souphanouvong. The disastrous failure of Katay's military campaigns against the Pathet Lao had caused his temporary downfall and Souvanna Phouma was in power again as prime minister. I had just come from Cambodia where the Head of State,

*A Thousand Days, pp. 324-25. Hereafter, all references to Schlesinger are to this book, with page numbers given in the text.

Prince Norodom Sihanouk, had told me in no uncertain terms that Cambodia absolutely rejected being placed within a SEATO "zone of protection."* Perhaps I would seek from Souvanna Phouma a similar statement of rejection of SEATO "protection"! Perhaps I had brought a message to facilitate contacts between the two half-brothers and get talks started again—the very thought of which sent temperatures mounting in the SEATO embassies. The atmosphere in the U.S. Embassy was panicky enough at the best of moments in those days, I was informed by a friendly colleague.

The previous ambassador, Charles W. Yost, had been whipped off to another post a few weeks earlier, because an FBI investigating team, checking on the reasons for U.S. diplomatic defeats in Southeast Asia, discovered that Yost's wife, of Polish origin, had been seen on several occasions speaking *in Polish* to members of the Polish delegation of the International Control Commission (ICC). At a diplomatic reception on the Saturday night of my arrival the U.S. Chargé d'Affaires had approached Katay, then vice-premier, and enlisted his support for my expulsion. Fate took a hand next morning when Katay was offered a ride on a pony belonging to the wife of head of the Canadian delegation to the ICC. Reluctant to admit that he was not a good cavalier, Katay climbed aboard and was promptly thrown, the pony galloping off dragging him behind with a foot caught in the stirrup. With body and pride badly wounded, Katay retired to his home town of Paksé in the South. At the Laotian foreign office on Monday morning (there had been no planes to take me away in between) the cancellation of my visa was said to have been a misunderstanding. The American Chargé was snubbed when he also called—while I was at the Foreign Ministry—to officially demand my expulsion. A scribbled note from an official and the police, smiles all over, restored my visa. I *did* see Souvanna Phouma. He *did* reject Laos being

*At one of its first sessions, the SEATO powers had included South Vietnam, Laos and Cambodia in a SEATO "zone of protection" without consulting the governments of those countries.

placed under SEATO protection; he *did* inquire as to Souphanouvong's health and expressed the hope that negotiations would soon get under way again.

Katay's accident removed him from the scene for a critical two weeks during which arrangements were finalized for the meeting between the two half-brothers to end the civil war. The first such meeting was in July 1956, following the arrival of Souphanouvong at Vientiane. Battlefield activity ceased completely and by the end of 1956 agreement had been reached on all points under discussion. The Neo Lao Haksat would start functioning as a normal political party; its representatives would be included in a new coalition government of national union pending nationwide elections; Laos would adopt a policy of neutrality based on the five principles of peaceful coexistence and "would not adhere to any military alliance and not permit any country to set up their military bases on Laotian territory apart from those envisaged in the Geneva Agreement." (This proviso related to some small French training installations.)

The agreement marked a severe setback to the first U.S. attempt to install and consolidate a puppet regime in Laos. J. Graham Parsons, who succeeded Yost as ambassador to Laos, was later to testify before a U.S. congressional committee: "I struggled for sixteen months to prevent a coalition" (as mentioned by Hilsman, p. 118). He failed temporarily at least but continued the battle as Under-Secretary of State for Far Eastern Affairs.

4

The Second Round

Agreement was one thing, but getting it implemented was quite another. Good agreements have never been lacking throughout the whole history of the Laotian problem, but any that implied real national reconciliation and real independence were sabotaged by the United States. The Souvanna Phouma-Souphanouvong agreements had to be ratified by the National Assembly and the U.S. Embassy launched a vigorous campaign to prevent this. Every member of the National Assembly was visited by Embassy personnel armed with fat pocketbooks; where bribes failed, blackmail and threats were used. While this campaign was in full swing, I made a second visit to Vientiane, in mid-January 1957. Souphanouvong, whom I had hoped to see had returned to his Sam Neua headquarters to make arrangements for Pathet Lao participation in the new government. The American and British embassies took advantage of his departure to step up their pressure on Souvanna Phouma to repudiate the agreements. I arrived with a visa valid for a week but which was again canceled and I was ordered out within 24 hours.

An American colleague from the Scripps-Howard newspapers who had fixed a luncheon appointment turned up red of face and apologetic: "I can't be seen talking to you," he explained, without even sitting down. "I wish I could stir up the sort of sensation in our embassies that you do by just being around." I asked what it was all about. "The Embassy says you are mainly responsible for bringing the two princes together again." And he took off, a frightened little man. Back at the hotel the police were waiting to ask when I was leaving. They spoke of a motorcycle "escort" to the airport.

A visit to the Foreign Ministry produced no results this

time. "There are forces stronger than we," was the apologetic reply. Souvanna Phouma sent a message by the Indian Chairman of the International Control Commission: "This time I can not help you. Come back after the coalition government is formed." The British ambassador protested to the ICC Chairman that it was "scandalous" that "such correspondents" could travel on the ICC courier plane—the only method of transport then, as now, between Hanoi, Vientiane and Phnom Penh. As an extra and revealing rebuke, the British ambassador added: "The job of the ICC should have been to keep those two princes apart instead of bringing them together." (This was because ICC transport had been used to shuttle Souphanouvong back and forth between his Sam Neua base and Vientiane. As all this was most strictly connected with the implementation of the Geneva Agreements the ICC was but performing its duty.)

The expulsion order was modified to enable me to leave on the next ICC flight for Hanoi which gave me time for a meeting with National Assembly deputies who told of the huge bribes being offered for a "No" vote on the agreements. Financial "aid" had been halted to back up the U.S. ambassador's threat that Congress would never approve funds to governments with "communists" in them. It took Nehru's personal intervention with Eisenhower to get the dollars flowing again.

Before I left, there was a curious and revealing incident. My wife, who had accompanied me on this trip, and I were having an aperitif in a small bar on the afternoon prior to our departure for Hanoi. It was deserted except for one other client. Although there were at least a dozen free tables, he staggered over to our's and asked, in an unmistakably American voice, if he could join us. I replied: "Frankly, no. We are here for a quiet chat and there are plenty more tables." He staggered off belching to another table, shortly afterward to collapse into a cycle ricksha, parked outside the bar, and appeared to go to sleep. When we called the barman waiter, a Frenchman, for the bill, he whispered from the corner of his mouth:

"He's not drunk. He's CIA. I know because I'm Deuxieme

Bureau.* Don't be fooled by him. Watch his car—he's got a special gadget in it."

By this time, the American had rolled out of the cycle into the driving seat of a jeep and seemed to be fumbling with the gears. As we stepped out onto the footpath the jeep leapt at us like a rocket. Had I not jumped and swung my arm to knock my wife back, we would both have been crushed against a stone wall adjoining the bar. As it was, the jeep made a crazy turn, lurched back on to the street and went roaring on its way. Had there been an "accident" the pretext would be "drunken driver"—who with diplomatic immunity could be flown out of the country to avoid even perfunctory court proceedings.

Next morning before the plane left we dropped into the bar again to thank the barman. "I don't know what you're talking about," he snapped, "and I've never seen you before."

Whether he was really "Deuxieme Bureau" or not, I shall never know, or why he should have taken the unusual step of revealing it, if he was. Perhaps it was because he wanted to add urgency to his warning. At that time, and ever since, the French were very hostile to American attempts to take over the country and as the chief American accusation against me was that I was responsible for "bringing the princes together" and supporting the "neutralists," the French had an interest in seeing that I was not bumped off by the CIA. The latter presumably knew we would be in the bar at that time, because we had fixed an appointment with another American journalist who did not turn up. As a similar jeep "accident" had occurred a few weeks earlier in Athens, in which a left-wing leader, Lambrakis, had been run down by a CIA agent, we considered ourselves fortunate to have escaped. Had we not been warned, and stepped straight out to the street which was the normal exit from the bar, we would have been crushed against a huge truck, parked a few yards ahead

*More or less the French equivalent of the CIA.

of the jeep. As it was, we left without further incident to return to our Hanoi base.

In March 1957, Prince Phetsarat returned after 11 years of exile and was immediately subject to the standard pressures of the U.S. and British embassies. There were great hopes among the latter that after so many years in Bangkok he would take a pro-SEATO line. A month after his return, although he had expressed the desire to live as a "simple citizen," the king restored his old title of Viceroy. This now had little meaning but it gave him the prestige of "elder statesman," a status which the pro-SEATO embassies were certain they could turn to their advantage. His first public statement horrified them. Phetsarat wholeheartedly approved the setting up of a coalition government and called for "absolute neutrality, clear and without hypocrisy," and as concrete expression of this he proposed the immediate establishment of diplomatic relations with Hanoi and Peking. A fascinating sidelight on his return and on his character was that he brought with him some modern printing machinery on which he hoped Vientiane's first daily would be published.

By one means and another the actual formation of the coalition government was delayed until August 1957, although neither bribes nor threats were able to block ratification by the National Assembly. Souvanna Phouma remained premier and took over the Ministry of Defense; Souphanouvong became Minister of Economic Planning, Katay Minister of the Interior and Sananikone Minister of Foreign Affairs. By November 1957 the Pathet Lao loyally wound up their administration in Sam Neua and Phong Saly provinces and handed them over to the royal government; members of the Pathet Lao forces were demobilized and went back to their native villages, all except those from two battalions which were to be integrated into the Vientiane army as intact units.

"Complementary" elections were to be held in May 1958 to fill about one third of National Assembly seats; with Katay as Minister of the Interior and any real electioneering banned on the grounds of "subversive propaganda" the results seemed a foregone conclusion. For the 21 seats at stake the Neo Lao Haksat, facing its first electoral test, presented only ten candidates. Nine were elected! Katay and his allies had 26 and four were elected. Sananikone's supporters did not win a single seat. But the Peace and Neutrality Party, headed by Quinim Pholsena and allied to the Neo Lao Haksat, won four out of five seats contested in addition to four seats it already held in the National Assembly. Out of 15 candidates presented for 21 seats the Neo Lao Haksat and its ally had won 13, and Souphanouvong won his seat in Vientiane with a greater margin than any other candidate. General elections for all 59 seats in the National Assembly were to be held the following year and it was clear to Washington that with the most scrupulous western concept of "clean elections" and even with Katay's dollar-greased electoral machinery, Souphanouvong and his allies would have a landslide victory. This would be pushing devotions to democratic processes too far!

It was clear that Katay's usefulness was coming to an end. Within a few weeks of the "complementary" elections a new gimmick with a new personality was introduced. This was the Committee for the Defense of National Interests, CDNI for short, formed by a group of fascist-minded officers, chief amongst them General Phoumi Nosavan.

Roger Hilsman's version of the situation written from "inside" Washington some years later does not differ too much from mine written from the scene at the time. Referring specifically to the elections, he comments, "There was much ineptness on the government side—they had run eighty-five candidates for the twenty-one seats at stake—but the significance of the election was clear." Members of the CDNI, "which everyone knew the CIA had sponsored" (indignantly denied at the time!) were very active, he observes. Referring to the concern of the U.S. Government, he says there were many who agreed with Parsons, now in Washington as Deputy Assistant Secretary of State for Far Eastern Affairs, who as ambassador had fought for "sixteen months to prevent a coalition. In any event," he continues "the United States Government reached a decision to hold up its monthly payment to the Lao Government—on the pretext that there was corruption in the commodity import program and a need for monetary reform."* With the CDNI and others making the most of the opportunity, "a parliamentary crisis quickly flared up and on July 23, they succeeded in swinging enough votes to cause Souvanna [Phouma] to lose a vote of confidence in the National Assembly and resign."

With Souvanna shipped off as ambassador in Paris, Phoui Sananikone formed a government that excluded the two Communist ministers (Souphanouvong, Economic Planning, and Phoumi Vongvichit, Education) "but did include four members of the CDNI who were not members of the National Assembly." Sananikone "then embarked on the policy of 'pro-Western' neutrality . . . and backed it up by putting an end to most of the abuses in the commodity import program, abolishing the license system, providing for American customs inspectors, and instituting an effective monetary reform" (pp. 117-18).

Schlesinger's account is even more forthright: "In 1958 Washington decided to install a reliably pro-western regime. CIA spooks put in their appearance, set up a Committee for the Defense of the National Interests (CDNI) and brought back from France as its chief, an energetic, ambitious and envious officer named Phoumi Nosavan. Prince Souvanna, who had shown himself an honest and respected if impulsive leader was forced out of office, a veteran politician named Phoui Sananikone took his place. In 1959 the State Department backed Phoui but the CIA preferred Phoumi" (p. 326).

It was an open secret in Vientiane that the U.S. Embassy paid 100,000 dollars a vote to bring down the coalition government, but it was typical of the weak, vacillating stand

*There was indeed corruption which the CIA had encouraged and deliberately used to build up a new compradore class fattening on U.S. aid. Katay ran a whole string of banks and import-export companies through which all U.S. aid was financed. But he had failed. Under the new system the dollars passed through Sananikone's hands.

that has marked the political career of Souvanna Phouma that he accepted defeat so easily and went off into exile in Paris. In the new government, Katay was given another chance to "redeem himself." With the ministries of Defense and Interior in his hands, the Pathet Lao forces disbanded, except for the two battalions, with their key cadres exposed in open and defenseless positions as integrated members of the administration, Katay was all set to prove his worth. Troops were sent to seal off the frontiers between Sam Neua and North Vietnam and the killings started. In Phong Saly not a single Pathet Lao cadre escaped. In the old resistance bases in Attopeu and Saravane, to which cadres had returned after the 1957 agreements, the heads of those murdered were publicly exposed to show the Pathet Lao had ceased physically to exist. Katay did not however have enough troops and police to concentrate them everywhere at the same time for the arrests and killings, and in some areas small groups of armed resistance started up again.

Throughout the latter half of 1958 and the beginning of 1959 the killings went on, Katay taking revenge for his defeats in 1955 by using his army and police against unarmed patriots who had devoted years to the independence struggle. On February 11, 1959 Sananikone denounced the Geneva Agreements and declared that as far as his government was concerned the ICC had ceased to exist. Demands by the Soviet Union, as Co-Chairman of the 1954 Geneva Conference, to Britain, as the other Co-Chairman, for the reconvening of the ICC, backed by Nehru (as India was Chairman of the ICC), went unanswered. Katay and Sananikone went ahead with plans for the final coup, the liquidation of the two Pathet Lao battalions.

On May 9, 1959 the battalions, which by that time had been separated—one of them stationed near Luang Prabang, the other on the Plain of Jars—were ordered to line up for the ceremony of "integration" into the Royal Army, without arms or uniforms, as they were to get new ones. At the same time units of the Royal Army with U.S. tanks and artillery moved in to surround them. The battalion commanders demanded time to get instructions from their leaders in

Vientiane. But by this time Prince Souphanouvong, Phoumi Vongvichit and other Neo Lao Haksat leaders had been placed under house arrest. On May 18, they were presented with an ultimatum to surrender or be wiped out. About one third of No. 1 Battalion escaped that night, despite an "eyeball to eyeball" encirclement. The following morning General Rattikone, commander-in-chief of the Royal Army came in person to receive the surrender of No. 2 Battalion— and found an empty barracks. Despite a frantic pursuit, with paratroop battalions dropped ahead of them and soundly thrashed, No. 2 Battalion and eventually almost half of No. 1, managed to march and fight their way back to their resistance bases in Sam Neua and Phong Saly. As revenge, Souphanouvong and the other leaders were removed from house arrest and flung into the Vientiane jail.

In Hilsman's version, No. 2 Battalion "taking the government forces completely by surprise—decamped to North Vietnam with all its equipment and dependents in a forced march from where it had been stationed on the Plain of Jars. . . . The Pathet Lao with Vietnamese help, then set about to drive out government forces and officials from the two provinces of Phong Saly and Sam Neua and to consolidate their control" (p. 120). Why on earth the Pathet Lao forces should first go to Vietnam, Hilsman does not explain. In fact No. 2 Battalion made an epic fighting march for almost one month from the Plain of Jars straight back to their former base in Sam Neua province, where they were received with open arms by the population. There they split up into small groups and engaged the Royal Army garrison troops in guerrilla warfare. Part of No. 1 Battalion managed to straggle back to Phong Saly to do the same thing, part were dispersed in Luang Prabang and neighboring provinces where they started guerrilla activities again in order to survive. Having dealt with the pursuing troops, thrashed five battalions, two of them crack paratroop battalions air-dropped in their pursuit, and fought their way out of several "steel ring encirclements," Battalion No. 2, about which Hilsman writes, had no difficulty in dealing with the demoralized troops in their home province of Sam Neua. But Hilsman, it seemed, had to throw in this absurdity to contribute to the official mythology of Vietnamese "aggression" in Laos.

The escape of the battalions was a horrifying blow to Sananikone, Katay and their CIA-State Department bosses. They had no illusions as to the fighting quality of the Pathet Lao troops nor as to the popular support they enjoyed throughout the country.

Phoui Sananikone, continued Hilsman, "asked for more American aid and more American military technicians and advisers and the United States agreed, announcing that it would send military technicians who would wear civilian clothes in token deference to the Geneva accords, to help in expanding the Royal Lao Army from 25,000 to 29,000 men" (p. 120).

Previous to this Hilsman had provided an example of the duplicity and hypocrisy with which Washington violated key paragraphs of the Geneva Agreements: "To accommodate to the Pentagon's insistence on having a Military Assistance Advisory Group (MAAG) in spite of the provisions of the Geneva Agreements, the State Department agreed to let one be set up in disguise. The PEO, for Programs Evaluation Office, was set up as part of the economic aid mission, and the military officers wore civilian clothes—to no avail, since the deception eventually became known and hit the newspapers" (p. 112).

Guerrilla warfare started up again in many parts of the country and mutual recriminations between Sananikone and the now rising star of the CIA, Nosavan, came to a climax at the end of 1959 when Sananikone kicked Nosavan and the other CDNI ministers out of his government. (Katay suddenly took ill and died at the end of December 1959.) Within 24 hours, on New Year's Eve, Nosavan carried out a military coup and swept Sananikone out of office. This was the real start of the Nosavan era. Washington had found another "strong man":

"During early 1960," writes Schlesinger, "Phoumi [Nosavan] dominated non-communist Laos. Recognizing that Defense and CIA were committed to him, he felt free to ignore their advice, rigging the spring elections so blatantly, for example, that the results lacked any color of legitimacy" (p. 326). The Pathet Lao which had dominated the "complementary" elections a year earlier were wiped off the slate. Hilsman points out that in Sam Neua province, a home base for the Pathet Lao and "virtually inaccessible" to the Vientiane government "the Pathet Lao candidate was supposed to have received only thirteen votes out of over six thousand cast." All seats were won by Sananikone and the CDNI!

Meanwhile in his solitary prison cell in the outskirts of Vientiane, Souphanouvong had been working on the prison guards, awakening their patriotism, appealing to their conscience, gradually establishing human contact—very difficult at first because the guards had strict orders not to exchange a word with their captives and to cover their ears if addressed. In March 1960, Prince Phetsarat died, but younger brother Prince Souphanouvong was not permitted to attend the funeral. Souvanna Phouma returned for the occasion but was not permitted to see his half-brother. At preliminary hearings, the judges could find no pretexts to condemn Souphanouvong and the others. (One judge was so impressed with Souphanouvong's bearing and arguments that he later joined the Pathet Lao.) Early in May 1960, the prisoners were tipped off that there would be no trial but that they were to be "shot while attempting to escape" during a supposed transfer to another prison. Shortly after this news, at dead of night, Souphanouvong led all 16 out of prison, together with nine prison guards on duty that night, all of them armed and disguised in M.P. uniforms. Eight of the guards had been won over by Souphanouvong's appeals, the ninth, in charge of the arsenal, decided "to go along" after explanations from the others. Following on the escape of the Pathet Lao battalions, this was too much. "Strong man" Nosavan ranted and raved and pledged to deliver the escapees dead or alive—and certainly it would have been dead.

Virtually the entire Laotian army and police, complete with U.S. advisers were mobilized in pursuit.*

Souphanouvong and his comrades were terribly weakened from their year in prison. It was the start of the rainy season. Their route lay over series of jungle-covered mountains, 300 miles back to Sam Neua. To avoid reprisals on villages they slept in the open, soaked to the skin, plagued by leeches and mosquitos. But they evaded their pursuers, handed back from unit to unit by guerrillas who by that time were already organized even in the areas adjoining Vientiane province.

The whole story of the escape and the ideological preparatory work done by Souphanouvong in the seemingly impossible conditions of his imprisonment, is a worthy theme for a great novel of human adventure and courage, a thriller which no imagination could improve on. Once again it testified to the extraordinary qualities of this prince turned revolutionary. And not even Hilsman could invent a Vietnamese angle to this one!

One morning, some three months after the escape while they were still far (two months in time as it later turned out) from their Sam Neua base, Souphanouvong switched on his transistor radio to hear the electrifying news of a military coup in Vientiane, pulled off by an unknown paratrooper, Captain Kong Le. Unknown, that is, to the outside world and most Laotians.

Souphanouvong knew who he was and so did Singkapo,† listening to the radio at his side. Kong Le came from the same village as Singkapo and had studied under the latter in the village school. Later when Singkapo had established his reputation as one of the most brilliant of the Pathet Lao commanders, the CIA chose Kong Le—by then an American-trained paratroop officer—to approach his former teacher and

---

*I have described the escape in more detail in *The Furtive War*, Chapter 10.

†Colonel Singkapo Chunamali Sikhot, member of the Central Committee of the Neo Lao Haksat and head of the Pathet Lao armed forces.

try and win him over. In a series of discussions that lasted over three months it was Singkapo who persuaded Kong Le of his real duties as a patriot. At their last meeting Kong Le said: "When the right time comes you may find support from unexpected quarters. Many of us are sick of this business of killing our brother Laotians."

Later, at the time of the escape of the Pathet Lao battalions, after the crack 1st Paratroop battalion sent in pursuit had been badly defeated, Kong Le's 2nd Paratroop battalion was ordered into action. He managed to get a message to Singkapo in prison, asking for advice. Singkapo said he had no alternative but to go and advised him "not to expose yourself or the battalion too much." Kong Le was slightly wounded at the first contact, and demanded hospitalization. Without him to lead, the battalion fled at the first real fire fight and was withdrawn for garrison duty as punishment.

In their jungle hide-out, Souphanouvong and the others discussed the situation. Once the details became clear, it was decided that Singkapo should return with utmost speed and join forces with Kong Le. He covered the distance that had taken three months during the escape in seven days, to a point close enough to Vientiane for Kong Le to send a helicopter to pick him up.

The coup took place on August 10 and at a public meeting two days later Kong Le declared: "Many past governments promised to follow a neutral course but they never kept their promises. My group and I are ready to sacrifice everything including our own lives in order to bring peace and neutrality to our nation." The king invited Souvanna Phouma, home on leave from Paris, to form a new government, which he did, but with his usual genius for vacillation and dangerous compromise he brought in Nosavan as Deputy Premier—and as Minister of the Interior of all posts. This government was recognized by the United States amongst most other countries of the world.

The second round had come to a close with Kong Le's coup, the climax to a whole series of shattering defeats for U.S. policies in Laos.

5

Out Into the Open

If Souvanna Phouma had displayed anything like the backbone of Kong Le at that time, he would have arrested Nosavan instead of accepting him into the government. With the joint strength of the Pathet Lao forces and units loyal to Kong Le, he could easily have done so. That the people would have supported such a move was certain. Indeed, as Hilsman comments:

"Phoumi [Nosavan] did not really intend to live up to the agreement, apparently having made it only to gain time. He almost immediately went to Savannakhet, his old home base, and began to seek support for a counter-coup from his relative, Marshal Sarit [Thanarat] of Thailand, and from Americans who represented agencies [!!!] likely to be sympathetic" (p. 123). An air-lift of American arms was started to Savannakhet while Thai units massed on the Thailand side of the Mekong, opposite Vientiane.

The Kong Le coup really caught the U.S. Embassy where it hurt most, knocking the wind right out of the policy experts. The effect was even worse because it came just one week after a new ambassador, Winthrop G. Brown, had arrived in Vientiane. Coming as the climax to a succession of defeats, some U.S. agencies were beginning to wonder which horse to back. Despite the fact that the new government, headed by Souvanna Phouma, was given official recognition by Washington, it was soon apparent that this was only to gain a breathing space and the real policy was to work for its overthrow.

On September 10, 1960 Nosavan set up a "Revolutionary Committee" headed by the well-known "revolutionary,"

Prince Boun Oum of Champassac! The latter thus made his grand debut on the world diplomatic scene as a leading protegé of the U.S. subversive affairs department. While arms poured into Savannakhet from Thailand, a blockade of supplies of any kind was imposed by Thailand against Vientiane.

Faced with Nosavan's hardly concealed plans for a march on Vientiane, Souvanna Phouma turned again to the Pathet Lao with an offer of participation in a new government of national union. In October, former Ambassador Parsons (then Assistant Secretary of State for Far Eastern Affairs) was dispatched to Laos to cope with the new horrifying turn of events. Kong Le had been an all-American manufacture. To Parsons' primitive political mind he had now turned "communist" and Souvanna Phouma was about to turn the same way! To mark the point, Parsons' arrival coincided with the cancellation of the U.S. monthly pay cheque to the Laotian army. According to both Hilsman's and Schlesinger's versions, Parsons demanded that Phouma should break off negotiations with the Pathet Lao, form an alliance with Nosavan and move the capital from Vientiane to Luang Prabang. (And pave the way for a Nosavan-Thai assault against what could be categorized as a "red bastion" once Souvanna Phouma had abandoned it.) Souvanna Phouma refused. Parsons left determined that Phouma had to be destroyed together with the capital. According to the Hilsman version, Ambassador Brown, slightly more sophisticated than Parsons, accompanied the latter to Bangkok pleading for a slightly more subtle play.

When Brown returned to Vientiane—to continue with Hilsman's account—he pointed out to Souvanna Phouma that "while the non-communist forces quarreled among themselves, Laos might well be lost to the Pathet Lao, who had followed their usual course of guerrilla nibbling while the negotiations were going on. The United States, Brown went on, would be willing to resume its financial payments to Souvanna if he in turn would not object to a resumption of U.S. deliveries to Phoumi [Nosavan]. The United States,

Brown was able to say, had Phoumi's promise not to use the
aid against Kong Le and the neutralist forces in an attempt to
bring down Souvanna Phouma, but only against the Pathet
Lao."

Both Souvanna Phouma and Phoumi Nosavan behaved
predictably. Perhaps nothing is more illustrative of the real
role of Souvanna Phouma than his gradual shift from
pro-French liberal-nationalism to pro-U.S. anti-nationalism.
"Souvanna Phouma quickly agreed," relates Hilsman, "hoping for one thing to finally convince the United States
Government that he was not so naive about the Communists
as they believed" (p. 125).

I do not believe that the Pathet Lao leaders or Kong Le
knew at that time that Souvanna Phouma had moved so far
to the right, that objectively he was already playing the U.S.
game and was ready to betray his closest allies.

As for Phoumi Nosavan, he acted with his usual treachery
and his contempt for those stupid enough to believe his
promises. "Phoumi violated the agreement," writes Hilsman.
"Over the next weeks as his military strength built up, it
became increasingly clear that Phoumi was moving his forces
into position for an attack on Vientiane" (p. 125).

Part of Nosavan's forces moved up from Savannakhet in
U.S. trucks, others were moved through Thailand to attack
Vientiane from across the Mekong. "Phoumi marched on
Vientiane and with plans drawn up by his American advisers,
won the only military victory of his life," is Schlesinger's
terse account of what happened (p. 328). (In two previous
battles, Kong Le had inflicted heavy defeats on Nosavan's
troops at Paksane and a still heavier one was inflicted by the
Pathet Lao No. 2 Battalion in Sam Neua.)

Kong Le's troops and the Vientiane population to whom
arms had been distributed fought very well. It took Nosavan's
forces 18 days to occupy the city, a decisive element in his
favor being artillery fire from the Thai side of the Mekong,
directed by U.S. helicopters hovering over the city. Charac-
teristically, Souvanna Phouma flew off to Cambodia as soon
as the fighting started. When it was all over Boun Oum moved

into Vientiane and renamed his "Revolutionary Committee" a government, which the United States promptly recognized as the authentic government of Laos.

In Phnom Penh, Souvanna Phouma lamented that he had been cruelly cheated by that "most nefarious and reprehensible of men," former Ambassador J. Graham Parsons. Of course he did not reveal details of the cheating—that arms which he had thought would be used *only* against the Pathet Lao had been turned against him. There had been a good deal of "cruel cheating" all round—Brown's and Parsons' cheating of Souvanna Phouma and Nosavan's CIA-sponsored cheating of everybody, and Phouma's own implicit cheating of the Pathet Lao and Kong Le, whose armed forces and the people of Vientiane had to suffer the consequences. Above all it was the Laotian people who were being most "cruelly cheated" by Washington policy-makers in a most ruthless display of power politics to bring a small Asian nation to its knees.

Kong Le's troops withdrew in good order and, supported by Singkapo's Pathet Lao forces, carried out a beautifully coordinated action to seize the Plain of Jars on New Year's Day, 1961, causing more howls of pain from Vientiane and Washington. This was another body blow. The Pentagon infinitely would have preferred to lose Vientiane than the Plain of Jars. Adding insult to injury was the fact that Kong Le's troops were transported to the Plain of Jars in U.S. armored cars and trucks.

To explain away this defeat, Nosavan invented the myth of intervention by North Vietnamese battalions in a note to the UN. In his book on Laos* Hugh Toye, in describing Kong Le's advance on the Plain of Jars, writes: "He had abandoned his two guns en route and his striking forces consisted only of three parachute companies and some heavy mortars. Phoumi [Nosavan] however, announced that seven Viet Minh battalions had crossed the frontier and that two of them were approaching the plain. It was thus hardly surprising that the

Laos: Buffer State or Battleground, Oxford University Press, London, 1968.

main garrison there bolted almost as soon as Kong Le was within mortar range. ... Up to this point Kong Le had received little or no help from the Pathet Lao." Toye then makes the point that North Vietnamese support came only much later. In any case, at a Vientiane press conference a few days later, with Boun Oum and the diplomatic corps present, Nosavan had to admit that there was no evidence of "North Vietnamese battalions."

In reply to Nosavan's screams for help—either SEATO intervention which France was blocking, or direct U.S. intervention—Eisenhower sent half a dozen AT-28 planes, described as for "training only," and what were known as "white star" military adviser teams. One of these was attached to each of Nosavan's battalions, in flagrant violations of the Geneva Agreements. They were ineffective. Having no moral incentive themselves, they were unable to inject any morale into Nosavan's troops. They could not explain convincingly why Laotians should kill Laotians.

John Kennedy took over from Eisenhower at the White House, but that did not change anything in Laos. By the end of January 1961, Nosavan had concentrated 20 battalions, about half his armed forces at that time, in a major offensive to retake the Plain of Jars. But even the "white star" teams—the start of the application of American "special warfare" in Laos—were unable to speed up the snail's pace at which the reluctant attacker advanced. Schlesinger says they covered 65 miles in 29 days. They showed speed only in retreat, fleeing when the Pathet Lao and Kong Le troops counter-attacked.

The Pathet Lao guerrillas took advantage of Nosavan's troop withdrawal from other areas for the Plain of Jars offensive, to liberate most of lower Laos, including the area along strategic Highway 9, linking Savannakhet with the South Vietnamese port of Dong Ha. About this time, the British, foreseeing disaster ahead for Nosavan, began to show interest in the proposal to revive the ICC which they had scorned almost two years previously, although tacitly they had approved Sananikone's denunciation of the Geneva Agreements in February 1959.

Hilsman describes "long and agonizing" meetings which he attended at this time with Foreign Secretary Rusk, Defense Secretary McNamara, the CIA chiefs and others to decide what was to be done. Among the proposals was one to parachute a division of U.S. Marines onto the Plain of Jars. "We can get them in alright," General Lyman Lemnitzer, Chairman of the Joint Chiefs of Staff, is recorded as saying. "It's getting them out that worries me." Various other proposals were considered for Americans killing Laotians as the latter were refusing to do it themselves.

At a dramatic, televised press conference on March 23, against a background of military maps of Laos which presented Nosavan's defeats as proof of the "progress of Communist encroachments," Kennedy blandly asserted, as Schlesinger notes, that if the attacks did not stop, "those who support a genuinely neutral Laos will have to consider their response" (p. 333). As every top-ranking U.S. official who had anything to do with Laos from 1954 onward had subscribed to the Dulles concept of neutrality and neutralism as "dangerous and immoral," the Kennedy statement caused the raising of diplomatic eyebrows everywhere, not least in the SEATO capitals and in Vientiane itself. The President then flew off to a meeting with British Prime Minister Macmillan where the two agreed that only massive intervention or a speedy ceasefire could save Nosavan from complete collapse. Rusk sounded out the possibilities of intervention at a Bangkok SEATO meeting, but was turned down again by the French.

Prince Sihanouk had long before proposed a reconvening of the Geneva Conference to discuss Laos and had been repeatedly snubbed by the United States and Britain for his pains. Now the British began to show interest in this idea coupled with a ceasefire. The U.S. ambassador to Moscow reported back that Khrushchev was more interested in Berlin than Laos and would not risk a fight there. (By this time diplomatic relations had been established between Laos and the Soviet Union which still recognized the Souvanna Phouma government.) Kennedy decided on a show of force to back up the various diplomatic moves he was then toying with. The Seventh Fleet was dispatched at full speed to the Gulf of Siam; helicopter units were shifted into northeast Thailand and a detachment of Marines was readied for action in Japan. All indications were that the United States was going to move into Laos in a big way. Kennedy spoke more and more of a "truly neutral" Laos in keeping with the old British diplomatic axiom, "If you can't stop it join it."

Doubtless under the influence of the Winthrop Brown-Souvanna Phouma conversation of the previous October, some of Kennedy's more sophisticated advisers were already working on the long-term idea of weaning the Souvanna Phouma neutralists away from the alliance with the Pathet Lao into which U.S. policy had pushed them—reluctantly as far as Souvanna Phouma was personally concerned.

By mid-April 1961, the net result of the series of events sparked off by the attempt to wipe out the two Pathet Lao battalions nearly a year previously, was that 70 per cent of the territory and about half the population of Laos was under the control of the Pathet Lao or the neutralists allied with them. All this was a predictable consequence of Washington's determination to stamp out not only "communism" but anything else in Laos which represented an obstacle to U.S. policies in the area. Official policy was to create an anti-communist, client state—which by definition would be anti-national and thus repugnant to the Laotian people.

Militarily the allied Pathet Lao and Kong Le forces could have pressed their advantage and driven the remnants of Nosavan's troops right back over the frontier to the training camps in Thailand from where many of them had come. On April 24, the USSR and Britain, as Co-Chairmen of the 1954 Geneva Conference, issued an appeal for a ceasefire which, for political reasons, the Pathet Lao accepted. It went into effect ten days later and the way was cleared for a new Geneva Conference. Had the boot been on the other foot and Nosavan about to deal a *coup de grace* to the Pathet Lao-Kong Le forces, the United States would certainly never have agreed to such a ceasefire and conference. The Pathet

Lao took into consideration the position of the socialist camp and the general line of peaceful coexistence.

In the meantime, there had been the Bay of Pigs fiasco in Cuba. Schlesinger reports that on April 20, in order that U.S. "restraint" in Cuba should not be interpreted as "irresolution everywhere," President Kennedy "transformed the corps of American military advisers in Laos, who up to that point had wandered about in civilian clothes, into a Military Assistance and Advisory Group, authorizing them to put on uniforms and accompany the Laotian troops. Later that day," continues Schlesinger in an interesting sidelight on Nixon's natural reactions in such situations, "when Nixon saw the President and urged an invasion of Cuba, he also urged a commitment of American air power in Laos" (pp. 336-37).

At the very outset of what was to be the long drawn-out Geneva Conference, it was clear that the U.S. and Boun Oum-Nosavan delegations were going to use the conference table to play for time while their armed forces were built up and prepared for another round on the battlefield. Due to open on May 12, the first session was delayed for four days because the U.S. delegates refused to sit down with the Souvanna Phouma-Pathet Lao delegation. It was delayed another six weeks, when the Boun Oum-Nosavan and Thai delegations also refused to sit down with the Pathet Lao. This was part of the crude tactics of trying to win the "respectable" Souvanna Phouma away from his "red" allies. Heading the Boun Oum-Nosavan team was Phoui Sananikone whose performance at the 1954 Geneva Conference has already been mentioned.

In the meantime U.S. military aid poured into Savannakhet and a feverish effort was made to re-form, reequip and reinforce Nosavan's shattered units. Despite the ceasefire, nibbling attacks were made during the latter half of 1960 to try and retake some of the strategic points lost during the February-March fighting, with uniformed U.S. "advisers" ostentatiously taking part.

With many stops and starts—stops while Nosavan's forces launched attacks, starts when the attacks were blocked and more time was needed for buildups—the Geneva talks slowly ground forward, at least as far as paper agreements were concerned. The declared aim of the participants was to end the civil war, establish national harmony and the unity of the country by setting up a new coalition government, representative of all trends. Agreement on setting up a coalition government was reached; it was also agreed that it would adopt a policy of neutrality. But because Nosavan, thoroughly discredited as he was by his treachery and military debacles, wanted to dominate the scene and continue to play the "strong man" in Laos, no progress could be made on the actual composition of a coalition government. He either wanted no coalition at all, or one under his leadership. And despite the official U.S. position of wanting a "truly neutral" Laos, Nosavan was backed to the hilt by the CIA and State Department.

Hilsman, maintaining the official pretense that Kennedy was having real difficulties in controlling such a puppet, confirms at least that it was Nosavan and not the Souvanna Phouma and Pathet Lao delegations who was responsible for the difficulties at Geneva.* "The Americans' troubles were with Phoumi [Nosavan], and they were very public indeed. As most of the great powers in history have discovered," he continues "a small and relatively weak ally can be powerful in stubbornness. . . . General Phoumi Nosavan was as clever in these matters as the others (Chiang Kai-shek, Syngman Rhee, Ngo Dinh Diem) had been. . . . If the United States took too strong a stand against the Communists, and Phoumi decided that there was no risk at all that the United States would abandon Laos, his course of action was obvious. He would adamantly refuse to negotiate with Souvanna for a coalition government and wait for an opportunity to provoke a Communist attack and so trigger an American intervention."

---

*A strikingly similar situation later arose in Paris at the end of 1968, when the Saigon regime with obviously strong backing from influential circles in Washington, was able to block the start of the quadripartite talks on Vietnam and when they finally did start, was able to block any progress because Washington wanted it that way.

(Which is precisely what Nosavan did in early 1962, with U.S. "advisers" in command.)

Hilsman then talks about deliberately "ambiguous" U.S. statements formulated so Nosavan could not be certain of the extent of support. "But Phoumi was undeterred and promptly set about to resist all pressures to participate in a coalition government. For he already had the experience in 1960 of forcing the United States to back down and bend to his will when he had marched on Souvanna's government after the Kong Le coup. And he undoubtedly also believed that this time, as in 1960, there would be a policy struggle in Washington in which he could count on the support of both the Pentagon and the CIA" (pp. 136-37).

At the end of February 1962, I flew into the Plain of Jars where the Souvanna Phouma-Pathet Lao coalition government had set up its capital at Khang Khay. It was one of those many periods in which the Geneva Conference was in recess. An hour before my plane touched down, Souvanna Phouma had flown in from Vientiane, from a meeting which the British and American ambassadors had arranged with Nosavan. "If you come to Vientiane and talk things over with Nosavan, all will be well," he had been assured. He was in a bad mood when he returned, frustrated and humiliated. No one had met him at Vientiane airport. He had to look for a hotel room like any ordinary tourist. Nosavan kept him waiting for several days while the U.S. Ambassador subjected him to a war of nerves by threatening SEATO intervention unless Phouma agreed to give Nosavan "at least" the ministries of Defense and Interior in any coalition. Nosavan asked for just this when they finally met.*

Washington was making a big pretense at pressures on Nosavan at this time and much publicity was given to the fact that the five million dollars monthly cheque for the Boun Oum regime was being withheld because of Nosavan's intransigeance. I found no one in Khang Khay who believed this. I asked Souvanna Phouma's acting premier and finance

*I reported this at the time; also see *The Furtive War*.

minister, Khamsouk Keola, what he thought about this. He laughed: "It's just a ruse. The American's give extra money to Nosavan's uncle, Marshal Sarit Thonarat in Thailand and he just passes it on. If the Americans want to put real pressure on, why don't they cut the arms supplies." Jacques Nevard, the *New York Times'* Vietiane correspondent, made the same point in a dispatch to his paper (February 22, 1962). After mentioning the reported halt in financial aid, he continued: "However, the United States has continued its military aid to General Phoumi Nosavan's forces. Weapons, ammunition and fuel have not been cut off. An airlift chartered from the Chinese Nationalists still functions. Uniformed teams of United States military advisers continue to serve with most of General Phoumi Nosavan's battalions in the field. . . . The general has placed more obstacles in the way of a coalition regime than any other leaders in the country."

When I discussed this with Prince Souphanouvong, he pointed out that U.S. military aid to Thailand had doubled since the ceasefire agreements were signed. "Why?" he asked. "Is Thailand at war? Deliveries include jet planes. Why? Either to help carry on an existing war or to start a new one. I have signed three agreements since the start of the Geneva talks. All I ask is that the other side honors their signatures. Now the Americans say they are ready to support a neutral government. We see no neutral attitude from them, only their policy of aggression." He listed the three agreements as one signed at Zurich, June 22, 1961 between himself, Princes Souvanna Phouma and Boun Oum on the setting up of a provisional coalition government of national union; another at Hin Heup, in Laos, on October 8, between the same three princes agreeing that Souvanna Phouma would be prime minister and that the government would include eight neutralists, four Pathet Lao and four Boun Oum nominees; and the third at Geneva, January 19, 1962 on the specific personalities to form the cabinet, which was repudiated within 48 hours by Nosavan. All these were within the framework of the Geneva Conference.

As for the "stopped pay cheque," the London *Times* reported much later (May 24, 1962) that the CIA provided the funds for Nosavan from "its own capacious budget. The belief is that the agency transferred the money from its operations in Siam."

By this time the United States had moved into "special war" in South Vietnam. Helicopter and air crews had started arriving in November-December 1961 and a U.S. command had been set up under General Paul Harkins in Saigon in February 1962. The fact of military intervention in South Vietnam could not but have its effect on the conference on Laos and the validity of any agreements reached. Such a monumental violation of the 1954 Geneva Agreements boded ill for whatever new agreements were reached at the 1961-62 Geneva conference on Laos.

A pet U.S. project was already being discussed in the press—to open up Road 9 in the South and drive a corridor to link the northern part of South Vietnam to Thailand through lower Laos by which troops and supplies could be shuttled back and forth as the military situation required. What was being presented to the outside world as a Nosavan-CIA rebellion against official policy was merely an attempt to implement Pentagon planning with the knowledge and approval of the President of the United States. The official support for a "neutral" Laos, like the pressures on Nosavan, were so much shadow play for public diversion. The pretended flirtation with neutrality was at a time when the United States was publicly condemning ideas for neutrality in South Vietnam—where advocating neutrality was a "crime" punishable by death—and was publicly rejecting Prince Sihanouk's requests for recognition of Cambodia's neutrality. Real U.S. policy was the one that Laos got from Nosavan, his generals and CIA advisers, not the prattle about a "truly neutral" Laos.

I asked Kong Le and Singkapo, at the time both holding the rank of general and heading the Joint Supreme Military Command, about the military situation. They explained, over maps, that in the three previous months Nosavan's forces had launched three major offensives, retaking some 1,800 square miles of territory. Nosavan had "simply walked out of the Na Mone (near the Plain of Jars) conference which was to pinpoint the ceasefire line and never came back," Singkapo said.

According to the situation on the military maps, it was clear that Nosavan was heading for a disaster. Since early January 1962, a striking force of 20 battalions had pushed some 70 miles behind the ceasefire lines in the northern sector to capture the small towns of Nam Ho, Nam Seo and Muong Houn. The Pathet Lao-Kong Le forces counterattacked, recaptured the towns, hurling the attackers back in disorder. Nosavan had ordered them to regroup in a valley, about ten miles east of the town of Nam Tha, the latter in Nosavan's hands on the edge of what should have been the ceasefire line. I described the situation at that time as follows:*

"A glance at the military map showed all the best of Nosavan's forces bottled up in a Dien Bien Phu situation, and almost all of the U.S. supply resources tied up, feeding them . . . 7,000 of Nosavan's elite troops, surrounded in a valley on Souvanna Phouma's side of the ceasefire line, an important proportion of his total fighting strength. After all, it was the loss of only 16,000 elite French troops at Dien Bien Phu that caused the collapse of their whole military effort in Indochina."

Singkapo and Kong Le decided to leave them there for the time being to "wither on the vine," hoping this might change Nosavan's arrogant obstruction to the formation of the coalition government. Cold, hunger and sickness had their effect as weeks dragged on into months and the besieged troops were not relieved. They were being supplied from a forward airfield at Muong Sin, about 60 miles from Nam Tha valley. This was the situation at the time I left Khang Khay in early March.

*In newspaper articles and in my book, *The Furtive War*, from which the passage is taken, p. 204.

Souphanouvong later told me the sequence of events which led to another great crisis and display of Kennedy brinkmanship. Early in May, the half-starved garrison at the Muong Sin airfield revolted. Troops were flown in to quell the revolt but the first plane that landed was immediately surrounded by the mutineers. There was a brief skirmish. Part of the reinforcements joined the revolt, others resisted and were killed, the plane destroyed. No other planes dared land. When news of this reached the encircled troops at Nam Tha, they realized their last hope of relief was gone and that their meager air-dropped supplies would be still further reduced or stopped altogether. They made a desperate attempt to break out to the West. Nosavan sent a relief force but it was ambushed before it could effect a junction. Those who managed to escape the encirclement fled in disorder toward the Mekong, joined by the panic-stricken garrison of Nam Tha town which had never been threatened during the four months' siege of the troops in the valley. The fleeing troops, officers and all, crossed the Mekong into Thailand, abandoning lots of equipment including plenty of Nosavan's artillery. It was Nosavan's greatest military debacle.

News of the four months' siege of Nam Tha had been ignored by the outside world and the debacle was presented as some sudden Pathet Lao-Kong Le violation of the ceasefire agreements. The Seventh Fleet and Marine units were again rushed to Thailand and all-out U.S. intervention was threatened.

Schlesinger and Hilsman give contradictory accounts of how the crisis developed which, if they are based on CIA reports, makes it clear that the White House was being just as badly informed by the CIA on Laos as it was on Cuba at the time of the Bay of Pigs shambles.

"No sooner had Phoumi [Nosavan] declared a readiness to negotiate than the Pathet Lao broke the ceasefire in a major way," reports Schlesinger, and continues, "On May 6, with North Vietnamese support, they seized the town of Nam Tha, where Phoumi had imprudently deployed a substantial force. The engagement was, as usual, almost bloodless. The

Royal Laotian army fled, and the communists appeared to be starting a drive toward the Thai border. This flagrant violation of the cease-fire brought a prompt reaction in Washington" (p. 516).

According to Hilsman, "in late January 1962, Pathet Lao and North Vietnamese troops closed around the capital of the province, the town of Nam Tha itself, digging in on the surrounding heights. . . . Over the next few weeks, against American advice, Phoumi flew in more and more of his troops to reinforce the Nam Tha garrison. By the end of January, five thousand of Phoumi's army, which by then totalled fifty thousand, were at Nam Tha, including important elements of his available artillery."

Why "against American advice"? In fact there were U.S. advisers with the Nam Tha troops which were flown in by CIA planes. Why did the troops have to be flown in if this was Nosavan-held territory? Hilsman does not explain. The explanation that the troops were bottled up in a valley, ten miles east of Nam Tha town, well behind Pathet Lao lines, is the logical reply. But Hilsman persists: "Still another attempt was made to persuade Phoumi to withdraw from the trap, but without success" (pp. 140-41). What trap could there have been except if Nosavan was operating in hostile territory? Hilsman does not explain. All he does is to try and disassociate the United States from the defeat.

"On May 2," Hilsman reports, "just 364 days after the cease-fire had been declared, one sector of the defense perimeter at Nam Tha received fire from the surrounding Pathet Lao and Vietnamese forces. The next day, twenty-five miles to the West, Communist forces attacked and captured the last remaining airfield in northern Laos, at Muong Sing. On May 4, they captured an outpost a mile and a half east of Nam Tha." (A very different version from that of a mutiny of Nosavan's forces on the airfield which would have been a logical consequence of the tactics that Singkapo and Kong Le told me they had decided on—to let Nosavan's forces "wither on the vine." Hilsman's account also differs from the "almost bloodless" action reported by Schlesinger and which tallies more closely with Souphanouvong's version.) "Then at 3 a.m. on May 6, four Vietnamese battalions launched an assault on the northwest segment of the defense perimeter and shortly thereafter, other battalions attacked from the east, northeast and southeast. The twelve Americans on the White Star team with the defenders reported that first one sector, then another had been overrun. At 7:30 a.m. the team itself was evacuated by helicopter. By nine that morning Nam Tha had fallen and the survivors among the Royal Army defenders were fleeing in disorganized panic down the road toward the Mekong and Thailand.

"Over the next three days the intelligence reports showed no further troop movement. The attack had been a large-scale probe, a major although still limited violation of the cease-fire" (pp. 140-41). The whole action fits perfectly into Hilsman's prediction, referred to earlier, that if Nosavan was sure of U.S. support he would "provoke a Communist attack and so trigger American intervention" (p. 137).

Apart from repulsing Nosavan's January offensive and blocking the "relief column," there had been no Pathet Lao initiative at all, nor did they pursue the fleeing Nosavan troops—although the temptation to deal a *coup de grace* must have been strong. Incidentally, neither Schlesinger nor Hilsman refer to the ambush of Nosavan's "relief force," either because the CIA did not report it, or because it would have too obviously revealed that it was Nosavan who had violated the ceasefire agreements by another attack into Pathet Lao held territory.

The allegation regarding Vietnamese troops was a throw-in line that neither author tries to substantiate. Other accusations that the attackers included Chinese troops were used as a pretext for fanning the fires of extended war, seemingly averted by the Kennedy-Khrushchev meeting in Vienna. My information based on the military maps I saw just prior to the battle, with the positions and designations of the opposing units clearly marked, was that the Pathet Lao forces on their own chased the rightist troops out of the Nam Tha area. Hugh Toye, with access to information from the "other side," in his book previously cited, confirms this: "The allegation that the Pathet Lao had been supported by Chinese troops was dismissed by the American advisers in the area. It was generally believed that there was at least a battalion of Viet Minh in Muong Sai, but many observers were satisfied that the Pathet Lao no longer needed even Viet Minh advice in order to deal effectively with their opponents. ... An American patrol 'back up the trail to Nam Tha found only scattered bands of Pathet Lao guerrillas and no Vietnamese'."

Whether there was "at least a battalion of Viet Minh at Muong Sai," I do not know; it would not have figured in the operational maps I saw. But it is true that some 2,000 U.S. military advisers were in Laos planning and supervising operations, including Nam Tha, as Hilsman's reference to the participation of the "white star" team indicates. It is also true that Thai and Kuomintang troops were operating under the CIA-Nosavan command.

It was the boomerang effect of the Nam Tha debacle and U.S. involvement in it that prompted the London *Times* dispatch referred to earlier, which put the blame on the CIA, as if it really did operate independently of the White House. Had the operation succeeded, like that against the Plain of Jars seven years later, there would have been no talk of "against American advice" nor of blaming the CIA.

Under the headline "CIA Is Blamed For Laos Crisis," the Washington correspondent of the London *Times* reported (May 24, 1962): "The Administration is now convinced that the Central Intelligence Agency has been up to its old devices again and must share a large responsibility for the situation in Laos. ... Apparently the evidence shows that the swarm of CIA agents in Laos deliberately opposed the official American objective of trying to establish a neutral government. They are believed to have encouraged General Phoumi Nosavan in the concentration of troops that brought about the swift and disastrous response from the Pathet Lao." The well-informed *Times* correspondent thus demolishes the myth that Nam Tha was "against American advice."

President Kennedy banged hard on the war drums and in

an exercise of brinkmanship which outdid Dulles at his worst, used Nosavan's defeat to step up the military occupation of Thailand (the Pentagon wanted support bases there for South Vietnam anyway.) The most important result however was that after a Kennedy-Khrushchev meeting in Vienna in the first week of June, another ceasefire was agreed, thus saving the rest of Nosavan's forces from complete destruction had the Pathet Lao decided to exploit the military situation. On June 12, agreement was reached on the composition of a coalition government. This paved the way for a reconvening of the Geneva Conference and the adoption of the documents now referred to as the 1962 Geneva Agreements on Laos. As for the government, I described it at the time as "a government of national coalition in which key posts are in the hands of Souvanna Phouma neutrals, some minor ones for the Vientiane neutrals whose 'neutrality' is of dubious hue, according to my informants, and the rest divided equally between the Neo Lao Haksat and Nosavan. The Neo Lao Haksat, in view of the major role they had played in defeating Nosavan and their long record of sacrifice and struggle for the real independence of their country, were extremely modest in accepting parity with Nosavan."*

The only reason that a ceasefire and coalition government were acceptable to Kennedy was that this was the only alternative to the complete destruction of Nosavan's forces.

Souvanna Phouma became Premier and Defense Minister, Souphanouvong Deputy Premier and Minister of Economic Affairs and Planning, Nosavan also Deputy Premier and Minister of Finance. Quinim Pholsena, a staunch pro-Pathet Lao neutralist, became Minister of Foreign Affairs. Such a coalition government could have been formed at any time during the previous eight years but for U.S. intervention. The presence of Nosavan in the cabinet justified suspicions of more storms ahead.

Another phase of the Laotian drama had come to an end. It was one in which the role of the United States in waging

The Furtive War, p. 206-07.

"special war" against the Laotian people had been smoked out into the open. Foreign military personnel were to be withdrawn after the signing of the Geneva Agreements which meant that the "white star" teams flew out to Thailand, got back into civilian clothes and flew back into Vientiane as embassy and AID personnel.

On paper the agreements looked good; it remained to be seen how they would work out. Hilsman ominously quotes Averell Harriman, who headed the U.S. delegation at Geneva, as stating around this time: "We must be sure the break comes between the Communists and the neutralists, rather than having the two of them teamed up as they were before" (p. 153). To bring this about now became the major aim of State Department, Pentagon and CIA.

6

Split and Kill Tactics

The most significant thing about the new coalition government on which the Laotian people and their well-wishers abroad had set their hopes, was that it never worked and never even started working. From the very first day it was a prisoner of Nosavan's troops and police who controlled Vientiane to where the former neutralist administration had transferred from Khang Khay for integration with the new administration. But it was Nosavan's placemen who staffed all the ministries and departments of the central government. Demands by Souphanouvong and the neutralists that the security and policing of the capital should be on the same tripartite basis as the coalition government itself, were ignored. Had Souvanna Phouma been prepared to take a strong stand on this, it could have been done. But his class interest prevailed and he seems to have been only too pleased to see the progressive forces frustrated and placed again at the mercy of U.S.-backed reaction. To have broken Nosavan's grip on Vientiane at this time, without the authority of Prime Minister Souvanna Phouma, would have meant restarting the civil war.

The new policy of weaning the neutralists away from the Pathet Lao, as a prelude to a renewed attempt to destroy first the latter and then the neutralists themselves, made itself felt from the very first days. Nothing worked. The coalition government was paralyzed. Economic plans, developed by Souphanouvong and approved by the National Assembly, were blocked by Nosavan as Finance Minister. Decisions taken by ministers were killed by vice-ministers or department chiefs on the CIA payroll. (It was subsequently revealed that

Nosavan had issued secret instructions that civil servants were to obey only orders from his old administration, on pain of severe punishment if they disobeyed.) There were mysterious "desertions" from Nosavan's troops to Kong Le's forces—not just a trickle of two's and three's but entire units at platoon and even company strength. Desertions in fact were at such a rate that the "desertees" were beginning to outnumber Kong Le's effectives in key areas. Repeated warnings to Kong Le himself had no effect; he seemed only too pleased to see his units strengthened in relation to the Pathet Lao.

Through bribery and flattery and by playing on his known weaknesses, Kong Le, now that he was back in Vientiane, was being "neutralized" in a special sense. He began to lose interest in his role and functions and during one critical period he faded out of the picture altogether, a moral or physical prisoner of Nosavan's men who even had infiltrated his headquarters. Strange orders were issued in his name. Suspicions among his subordinates hardened when some units were ordered in his name to evacuate key positions on the Plain of Jars, to be replaced by others who were in fact Nosavan's men in Kong Le uniforms. This seemed suspiciously like the trick with which Katay had tried to disarm the two Pathet Lao battalions.

Kong Le's second in command, Colonel Deuane, commander of the Plain of Jars-Xieng Khouang region, realizing what was happening, refused to budge. Souvanna Phouma, warned of the impending attempt at a takeover from within, brushed the warning aside as the product of Souphanouvong's "over-suspicious mind." This was the situation at the end of March 1963, with strong rumors of a coup at any moment in which the Pathet Lao and the left-wing neutralist leaders were to be assassinated. Vientiane itself swarmed with CIA agents at their usual work of trying to buy up or eliminate those they considered useful or dangerous.

On the night of April 1, Foreign Minister Quinim Pholsena, head of the Peace and Neutrality Party and one of the oustanding personalities in Laotian political life, was shot and killed with a burst of machine-gun fire as he walked up the steps of his Vientiane home with his wife, who was gravely wounded. They were returning from a reception at the Royal Palace. Within hours, the streets were filled with troops and tanks. Nosavan's forces tightened their encirclement of the city and one of the Kong Le units infiltrated by Nosavan "desertees" raced off to arrest Colonel Deuane as a prelude to taking over the Plain of Jars. Deuane's guards beat off the attack. A second assault next day, supported by seven tanks, fared no better, part of the attacking troops either refusing to advance or switching sides. Colonel Deuane was one of the most popular and efficient officers among the neutralist armed forces and the Kong Le elements among the attackers had no stomach for their task.

I met Madame Pholsena a few days after her husband's assassination. She had been left to bleed to death on the steps alongside her husband's body, refused any medical attention until Souvanna Phouma and Phoumi Vongvichit, the Pathet Lao Minister of Information, forced their way past Nosavan guards and insisted on her removal to a hospital. Her legs swathed in plaster from the hips down, she told me there was no doubt but that Nosavan and the CIA had arranged the assassination. She reminded me of what her husband had told me some months previously—that on a visit to the United States with Souvanna Phouma, highly placed agents made vigorous attempts to buy him over and had made all sorts of veiled threats when he scornfully rejected their offers.

The fact was that Pholsena had insisted on being present, in his capacity as foreign minister, at all discussions which Souvanna Phouma had in Washington, including the key meeting with President Kennedy. Souvanna Phouma had flown off to Washington a month after the coalition government was formed. He assured Kennedy that most Laotians preferred the United States to the Pathet Lao and agreed to Kennedy's demand that at all costs no U.S. military or economic aid should pass into Pathet Lao hands. A tacit agreement was reached that Phouma would do everything possible to limit, weaken and eventually eliminate Pathet Lao influence. It was highly embarrassing that Quinim Pholsena, a

man of known integrity and friendship with the Pathet Lao,
should be privy to such matters. Hence the all-out attempt to
buy him over, about which Pholsena had told me on his way
back from Washington. Very obstinate and capable, he was a
stumbling block to U.S. determination to win the neutrals
away from the Pathet Lao, so bullets were used where bribes
failed.

The actual killing was organized by General Sino, who
headed Nosavan's military police and had set up, under the
guise of a "National Security Coordinating Office" what was
really an assassination committee to eliminate the higher
cadres of the Pathet Lao and the progressive neutralists.
Another of the early victims of Sino's assassination teams was
Khan Thi Siphanthong, a colonel in charge of the neutralist
security services who was well aware of the details of Sino's
organization.

When the first attempt to seize or kill Colonel Deuane
failed and Kong Le's own troops refused further attacks, an
appeal was issued in Kong Le's name for help from Nosavan's
units. In the meantime, Souphanouvong and Phoumi
Vongvichit—with their experiences of May 1959 still fresh in
their minds—had slipped out through Nosavan's encirclement,
the former returning to Khong Khay, the latter to Sam Neua.
Nosavan's battalions moved up into the Plain of Jars, the
gates opened in certain places by Kong Le units which had
been most heavily infiltrated by the "desertees." But by
mid-April, when Nosavan's troops launched their attack, the
Pathet Lao forces had also moved up to support Deuane's
outnumbered units. Nosavan's men were beaten back easily,
except at one western outpost at Tha Thom which they were
able to overrun.

It is ironic to read Hilsman's account of this period. He is
obviously torn between showing his glee at the success of the
new policy and at concealing the truth as to how it was
implemented. After describing President Kennedy's acceptance at a National Security Council meeting of Harriman's
formula that "we must be sure the break comes between the
Communists and neutralists," Hilsman then pretends that the
Pathet Lao was responsible for the break:

"The Pathet Lao made their first move by attempting to take over Kong Le's neutralist forces. [In fact it was just this very close alliance that had most alarmed Washington.] When he inisisted on independence, they cut off the Soviet supplies coming to him overland from Hanoi. At Souvanna's request the United States stepped into the breach with a new flow of supplies through Vientiane." [This was simply a new version of the deal Souvanna Phouma had agreed to with Ambassador Brown behind the back of the Pathet Lao and Kong Le in October 1960, but directed exclusively against the Pathet Lao this time.]

"The Pathet Lao," continues Hilsman, "then began a more subtle but also more vicious campaign, in which Quinim Pholsena, nominally a neutralist, was the central figure. Quinim directed a network of secret agents in an attempt to subvert the more susceptible officers under Kong Le and to assassinate those who were loyal. The Communists had some success in their attempts at subversion, but when they assassinated Colonel Ketsana, Kong Le's courageous chief of staff, and an old friend, the neutralists closed ranks. [It was common knowledge in Vientiane that Ketsana had been assassinated by Nosavan's men after other efforts to turn Kong Le against the Pathet Lao had failed.] And they retaliated by assassinating Quinim himself. The Communists then tried an out-and-out military offensive against the neutralists. They attacked Kong Le's position on the Plain of Jars, driving him back into the western half of the plain. . . . Thus by the summer of 1963, the split was complete," Hilsman notes with satisfaction. "It was the Communists now who were isolated, and the non-Communist neutral and conservative factions who were joined in opposing them" (p. 153).

Indeed superficially it looked as if the Harriman formula and the tactics used to implement it had worked to perfection. But what the kill and split experts had overlooked was that the neutralists themselves were split—a very important part, those with real backbone, remaining true to the alliance with the Pathet Lao. Harriman and Hilsman were thinking exclusively in terms of the Vientiane political scene.

If the Pathet Lao were "isolated," they were isolated with the people, the most decisive form of "isolation" in the long run. Progressive and able neutralist leaders such as Colonel Deuane on the military side and Khamsouk Keola (minister of Health in the coalition government) on the political side remained firm. Their bases in the countryside were still solid. They had the support of the people everywhere, including Vientiane and other cities.

As for Kong Le, he later disappeared into exile and oblivion. He played his role in history in staging the 1960 coup. He could continue to play a role just as long as he remained true to his Pathet Lao allies, but no longer. In the end he realized the extent to which he had been tricked, used and then flung aside, once the CIA had squeezed him to the last drop of usefulness. The Pathet Lao knew how to utilize and develop all that was good in Kong Le, his patriotism and courage, and teach him the elements of people's war. The CIA knew how to utilize and develop all that was bad in him, especially his moral and ideological weaknesses.

Of the situation in April 1963, I wrote at the time that "the military plot failed due to the loyalty of Colonel Deuane and the main part of the neutralist forces in the Plain of Jars; to the reluctance of the Kong Le troops to attack their colleauges; to the vigilance of the Pathet Lao and to the low morale of Nosavan's forces. But it was a close call. Had 'Operation Trojan Horse' succeeded, the trap would have been sprung in Vientiane and all the Pathet Lao and progressive neutralist forces in the capital would have been caught in it.*

With the departure of Souphanouvong and Vongvichit from the capital the coalition government existed on paper only—to the jubilation of Washington. It was abundantly clear that Washington's policy, despite lip service to "neutrality," had never changed an iota. It was still dominated by the obsession of exterminating the Pathet Lao, the chief obstacle to their plans for the satellization of Laos. The process had

*The Furtive War, pp. 213-14.

started toward a polarization of two forces in the country instead of three. The rightists to which so-called "neutralists" like Souvanna Phouma had rallied; the leftists, comprising the Pathet Lao to which the progressive neutralists had now rallied.

By his failure to take the Plain of Jars, even with the advantage that treachery and surprise afforded, Nosavan had again proved his incompetence and his inability to inject any fighting spirit into the forces he had created. His star, like that of Prince Boun Oum—who had never played his role with much conviction or enthusiasm—was on the wane. Politically, Washington had somebody much more glamorous, Souvanna Phouma. Militarily, there was also something new in the air. The Royal Laotian Army, made up almost exclusively of the Lao Lum plainspeople, Buddhists who abhorred violence and whose hierarchy had a tradition of patriotism and thus supported the Pathet Lao, had proved in a dozen engagements that they had no stomach for killing fellow Laotians in the interests of a foreign power.

The conviction grew amongst U.S. military experts on the spot that it could never be converted into an efficient and reliable instrument despite the vast sums of dollars lavished on it. Something else had to be found.

Schlesinger reports that after Nosavan's 1961 fiascos, President Kennedy began casting around for new ways of fighting guerrilla wars. He decided on a vast expansion of the Special Forces as the best way to fight "special wars." Something really new had to be created "in order to confront the existing challenge of guerrilla warfare in the jungles and hills of underdeveloped countries. Over the opposition of the Army bureaucracy, which abhorred separate elite commands on principle, he reinstated the S.F. green beret as the symbol of the new force" (p. 341). Both Schlesinger and Hilsman make it clear that this decision was specifically related to the defeats of Nosavan's U.S.-trained forces in Laos.

It was to be expected therefore that Laos should be one of the first experimental fields for the application of this new weapon, which was to become an important auxiliary in carrying out self-appointed duties of the United States as the world's super-gendarme. Special Forces are local mercenaries under U.S. officers, trained and paid by the CIA. But how to get Laotians to perform any better under U.S. officers than they did under puppet Laotian officers? No progress was made until the Meo tribespeople came into the picture.

Because of their experienced exploitation of ancient tribal feuds and of traditional hostility between the tribespeople and the Lao Lum, the French had been able to build up a Meo commando force which totaled 3,000 by the end of the first Indochina war. They were headed by two opium-dealing tribal chiefs, To Bi and To Jeu. But the majority of the Meo fought on the side of the Pathet Lao, under the famous Meo chieftain, Faydang, today a member of the Central Committee of the Nao Lao Haksat. They still remain loyal to the Pathet Lao. But talent scouts of the CIA spotted the commandos left by the French and also one of their Meo officers, a lieutenant Vang Pao.

The CIA decided to take them over and use them as the nucleus for the Laotian Special Forces. Racially conditioned against the Lao Lum, they could be inspired with contempt equally against Souphanouvong and the neutralists, including Souvanna Phouma if necessary. Living on the summits of the mountains, the Meo tribes are very strategically placed for just those sort of nefarious activities that the Special Forces are trained to undertake. In Hilsman's muted account, "there were occasions of tension in 1962 and 1963 when it was useful to have the Meo blow up a bridge or occupy a mountain top as a move in the deadly game of 'signaling' that the United States had to play to deter the Communists from adventuring with the Geneva accords. But arming the tribesmen engendered an obligation not only to feed them when they were driven from their traditional homelands but also to protect them from vengeance" (p. 115).

By 1964, after Nosavan had suffered a further series of defeats in renewed attempts to take the Plain of Jars and to open up Route 9 in the South, the Americans were busy building up the original force of 3,000 Meos to 15,000 organized in five zones and 48 sectors in upper and lower Laos. At Long Cheng, southwest of Xiang Khouang, a big "hush-hush" base was developed, complete with aerodrome, officers' training school, supply depots and training centers for espionage, sabotage, signaling and all the cloak and dagger techniques in the Special Forces arsenal. The three zones in upper Laos were under the nominal command of "General" Vang Pao, the two in lower Laos under another tribal chieftain, Boun Pone. The real headquarters for planning, supplies, training and as a rear operations base was at Oudon in Thailand, known as HQ 333, and run directly by U.S. Special Forces. Another center for higher "studies" in sabotage was set up at Lopboury, also in Thailand, while the top experts were sent off for finishing courses in Japan and the United States itself. From scores of disillusioned Meos who have been captured or simply deserted when they found out what they were being used for, the Pathet Lao leaders soon constructed a detailed picture of how the Meo Green Berets were trained and organized.

Although the majority were Meos, the CIA recruited among Thais who had served in South Vietnam, Kuomintang remnants from Burma and Thailand, some in northern Laos also—a precious collection of killers, thugs and bandits.

Armed, equipped, trained, fed and paid out of the special CIA budget, they got more and better of everything, including pay, than the Royal Army troops. Anything that could be done to increase hostility between the Lao Lum and the tribes, the Royal Army and the Special Forces, was all to the good, as far as U.S. policy was concerned. A purely mercenary army was created which belonged entirely to the United States, the operational plans of which never had to be shown to the Vientiane government or its staff headquarters. More and more the Special Forces were built up not only as the main U.S. military instrument in Laos but as the main military force in the country. Money, as Senator Fulbright complained, was no object.

Anything needed to corrupt—booze, girls, opium—was available as rewards for the most odious crimes. Traditionally the Meos, like the other tribespeople, were exceptionally honest and straightforward, the most loyal of allies. Everything that power and wealth could furnish to break down their moral qualities was used to transform them into sneaks and liars, cheap assassins and bandits who grew to despise not only the Lao Lum and the other tribespeople, but also those of their own race who were not swaggering around in Special Forces uniforms.

Under the feudal relations which were still maintained among the tribes in the non-liberated areas, it was necessary only to corrupt the heads of the various clans and tribes and the young men were automatically obliged to follow their leaders. Without a sense of nationhood, many were thus dragooned into the Special Forces, and in training camps in Thailand were taught new ways of killing their compatriots, without knowing where they were or who was the enemy they were supposed to exterminate.

While this build-up of the Special Forces continued, Souphanouvong made many attempts to get the coalition government functioning again. He proposed, among other things, to transfer the administration to Luang Prabang, and to create a neutral zone around the royal capital, both zone and city to be policed by tripartite security forces. This was turned down, as were many other proposals, some of which had the support of the ICC, designed to create conditions of security in Vientiane itself to make the normal functioning of the coalition government possible. Until a minimum of security was guaranteed in Vientiane, Souphanouvong would not return to put himself and other Pathet Lao leaders in a trap which the rightists could spring at any moment they desired.

In April 1964, in response to an initiative of Souphanouvong, Souvanna Phouma and Nosavan came to the Plain of Jars to talk things over in a tripartite meeting. Nothing emerged from it, but the very fact that it took place shook the CIA. On April 19, just after the two returned to Vientiane from what was in reality a fruitless meeting, there was a military coup, carried out by General Kouprasith

Abhay, a relative of Phoui Sananikone, and as willing a right-wing puppet as Nosavan. Souvanna Phouma was placed under house arrest, Nosavan relieved of part of his command, and Kouprasith put himself at the head of a "Revolutionary Committee," acting as the new government.

Obviously the coup caused a commotion abroad, the ripples of indignation reaching up the Co-Chairmen of the Geneva Conference who expressed their disapproval, forcing the State Department also to make noises of dissent. President Johnson's special envoy, William Bundy, turned up in Vientiane on April 21 and doubtless received assurances that nothing had been agreed at the Plain of Jars conference with Souphanouvong. He then set about restoring order, in such a way that the coup-makers and CIA would be satisfied, but under a cloak of respectability that would look good to the Co-Chairmen and the outside world. There followed a whole series of maneuvers, in which the coup-makers agreed to accept Souvanna Phouma again as long as he "broadened" his cabinet. Nosavan was restored to his post as vice-premier, while Souvanna Phouma and Nosavan negotiated an agreement to fuse the neutralist and right-wing parties. The "broadening" of the cabinet meant the exclusion of the Neo Lao Haksat members and the appointment of a right-winger to replace the murdered Quinim Pholsena at the foreign ministry.

From May 7, 1964, the date on which Souvanna Phouma announced the shotgun formation of a new government, the tripartite coalition government ceased to exist and the 1962 Geneva Agreements were in effect null and void, the legal basis of the agreements shattered by Souvanna Phouma's abdication of his responsibilities. More than ever Phouma was in debt to Washington who had "rescued" him from political, if not physical, liquidation, and the Pentagon was not tardy in exacting repayment. Within ten days of the all right-wing government being formed, American jets started bombing the main Pathet Lao bases in the Plain of Jars, Sam Neua and lower Laos. Nosavan's force started new operations on several fronts, supported by U.S. tactical aviation. (These first raids were two months before the Gulf of Tonkin incident, the pretext for the first attacks against North Vietnam.)

Ostensibly these raids were directed at the so-called "Ho Chi Minh Trail," along which North Vietnam was supposed to be infiltrating men and supplies to the South. In fact they were aimed at giving tactical support to Nosavan's ground operations and at wiping out the main Pathet Lao bases. In relation to the start of these air operations, Hilsman reveals that shortly after President Johnson took over at the White House on the assassination of President Kennedy, and some time before Hilsman himself resigned in March 1964, Walt Rostow for the State Department proposed "gradual escalation" of the war in North Vietnam and shortly afterward the Pentagon and CIA put forward a program of "low-level reconnaissance" in Laos. This was supposedly because of increased use of the "infiltration routes." Hilsman shows that at the time the total supplies required by the NLF from outside South Vietnam were six tons per day and that even two years later, by which time their armed forces had trebled, the Pentagon estimate of their needs from outside the South was 12 tons per day. Hilsman also points out that the "infiltration" rate was lower in 1964 than the previous year and that it was lower in 1963 than in 1962.

The new president had been stimulated, it seems, by one of General ("Killer" as he was known to World War II correspondents) Lemay's characteristic contributions, "We're swatting flies. . . . Let's go after the manure pile."

"The proposal for low-level reconnaissance over Laos— with the implication that bombing would follow if targets were spotted [or if the low-level reconnaissance planes were fired on as was inevitable]—had been made before," writes Hilsman. "But Harriman, Forrestal and I had fought it steadily. In the first place, we were worried about the effects on Laos itself. The Geneva Agreements of 1962 had achieved a precarious neutrality for Laos that, so far, both sides had respected in its broad outlines. There was a *de facto* partition rather than an effective government of national union, but by and large the Communists had stayed on their own side of the line of partition. . . . But we were also worried about the effects of an escalation on the struggle in Vietnam as well." Hilsman then accuses the North Vietnamese of using Laos as an infiltration route to the South and holds that the bombings could have been justified on these grounds. "At least 5,000 men a month could be infiltrated over the Ho Chi Minh trails—over 60,000 a year. Yet from 1960 on, the monthly average had been only 650 and the yearly average only 7,850. *More important, the personnel were not North Vietnamese, but still only the pro-Communist Southerners who had gone north in 1954 and were returning to serve in the Viet Cong as cadre"* (p. 527).*

Hilsman and Harriman were against the bombings because, as Hilsman writes: "If we openly violated the Geneva Agreements, it would be politically easier for the Communists to violate them even more openly, actually increasing their infiltration through Laos. To Harriman, Forrestal and me the conclusion seemed obvious. If we raised the ante by bombing, the North Vietnamese would respond by increasing the use of the infiltration routes to include northerners" (p. 528). But the "ante was raised" and under the pretext of bombing infiltration routes, all Pathet Lao bases in the liberated areas were attacked from mid-1964 onward.†

Rivalries and mutual recriminations between the Sananikone and Nosavan cliques continued to develop, the prestige of Nosavan still declining because of the incapacity of his forces to win a single victory on the battlefield. Although he was no longer in charge of military affairs, part of the shame of the defeats rubbed off on him as the armed

---

*The italics are mine. Hilsman was referring to the 140,000 Vietminh troops, cadres and a few of their families, who had temporarily withdrawn to the North under the 1954 Geneva Agreements, and who were to return to the South after the 1956 general elections which were never held due to U.S.-Diem repudiation of the Geneva Agreements.

†Hilsman resigned in March 1964 because of disagreement with Johnson's insistence on "military solutions" in Laos and Vietnam.

forces were very much his creation. Souvanna Phouma kept reshuffling his cabinet, moving it further and further to the extreme right. In March 1965, the Nosavan-Sananikone quarrels developed into armed clashes. Nosavan lost as usual and fled the country, to seek refuge with his cousin, Marshal Sarit Thanarat, the dictator of Thailand.

As the war in South Vietnam escalated in February 1965 with the start of the systematic bombing of the North and a month later with the landing of the first U.S. combat units in the South, the Meo tribespeople found many of their mountain-top villages being converted into U.S. bases, helicopter fields and radar-relay centers for guiding Thailand- and Seventh Fleet-based planes to and from their bombing missions. (Seventh Fleet planes bombing deep inside North Vietnam flew on to bases inside Thailand, refueling and restocking to bomb again and return to the carriers.) A great effort was made by the CIA to establish a network of such mountain-top bases in the Pathet Lao areas, supplied by two airlines operated by the CIA out of Vientiane and Thai airfields. (AP reported on June 20, 1965 that a 35-plane squadron with U.S. pilots carried out the supply work at a cost of ten million dollars a year. The funds came from the CIA.)

Obviously once such bases were established behind their lines, the Pathet Lao did their best to eliminate them. This is one of the explanations for Hilsman's reference, quoted earlier, to the "obligation not only to feed them [the Meos] when they were driven from their traditional homelands but also to protect them from vengeance." Protecting them from vengeance, as we shall see later, meant dropping American Green Berets to help defend the bases and, when that failed, forcibly evacuating the tribespeople into concentration camp-type reservations in the Vientiane-controlled areas.

Although the policy of "split and kill" yielded certain fruitful results for U.S. policy-makers during the first couple of years after the formation of the coalition government, it also resulted in splitting the right-wing forces, as illustrated by the Sananikone-Nosavan clash and the flight abroad of

Kong Le when his forces were integrated against his will into the rightist army. On the other hand there was a consolidation of the Pathet Lao and its allies, helped in mid-May 1964 by an uprising of patriotic elements within the Kong Le neutralist armed forces, the insurgents immediately establishing contact with the Pathet Lao. The new reinforcements, added to those already rallied around Colonel Deuane and Khamsouk Keola facilitated the formation of an Alliance Committee of Patriotic Neutralist Forces which replaced the weak and vacillating neutralists of the Souvanna Phouma school, to become reliable allies of the Pathet Lao. The Alliance very quickly became an important new political force in the country.

Following more coups and counter-coups between supporters of Nosavan and Sananikone-Kouprasith in early 1965 and further shuffles to the right by Souvanna Phouma there remained only six of the 19 members in the original tripartite Coalition Government, which did not prevent Souvanna Phouma from claiming that he still headed the government based on the 1962 Geneva Agreements.

The use of the Vang Pao mercenaries, so clearly in U.S. pay, the ruthless destruction of villages by bombs and napalm from U.S.-piloted planes, and the abdication by Souvanna Phouma of any semblance of a neutral or even nationalist position heightened national consciousness to a degree never before known in Laos. The last illusions as to Souvanna Phouma and his role in the country's independence struggle were dissipated. By mid-1965, with the build-up of U.S. combat forces in South Vietnam, the merciless bombing raids on the North and outrageous intervention in Laos, the United States had become recognized as the inveterate enemy of the Indochinese people. Souvanna Phouma was recognized as its puppet.

7

Laos in the Seventies

Throughout 1969, the tonnage of bombs dropped on Laotian villages exceeded that dropped in any year on North Vietnam, more than on Nazi-occupied Europe in any World War II year. The only way to escape the bombs was to accept concentration camp life behind barbed wire, living off U.S. handouts. In many cases there was no choice. After the bombs and napalm, helicopters swooped down, Special Forces commandos landed, their M-16's blazing at any who ran. Survivors were flung aboard to be dumped in a barbed wire enclosure called "refugee camp." Any dazed victims of military age would soon find themselves in uniform, a gun in their hands, in due course herding other villagers into similar camps.

As the victims increased in numbers, "camps" were upgraded into "centers," the latter expanded into "unity villages." As these multiplied they were linked together to form "restoration zones" of which 22 had been formed by the end of 1969 over the length, if not the breadth, of the land.* Officially Vientiane claimed a total population of 500,000 in the "restoration zones" by 1970, a staggering figure considering the total population of the Vientiane-controlled areas was at most 1,500,000. "Unity villages" and "restoration zones" were obviously the Laotian equivalent of the notorious "strategic hamlets" and "prosperity zones" in South Vietnam—the solution devised by the U.S.-controlled

---

*Since 1961 the Pathet Lao and progressive neutralist forces controlled two thirds of the territory and half the population of Laos, the rightists controlling the towns and villages along the Mekong river.

regime of Ngo Dinh Diem for emptying the sea in which the Vietcong fish swam.

The same methods of "accelerated pacification" which horrified the world at South Vietnam's Songmy* were used against other "Orientals" in countless Laotian villages. As in South Vietnam also, the "unity villages" were set up on the perimeters of towns and bases along the main highways as "protective belts" to take the first shock of attacks by the Pathet Lao against the bases. The destruction of entire hamlets of recalcitrants to "encourage" their neighbors to move "voluntarily" was commonplace. Defoliant attacks against crops and orchards speeded departures or stressed the hopelessness of return.

"Get out of your villages or else . . . " was the threat contained in the air-dropped leaflets—sometimes before the bombs and napalm rained down, more often later—to warn villagers not to try and set up house elsewhere. In their air-conditioned villas, the American experts could rationalize that it was cheaper to dump surplus U.S. rice and a few cases of condensed milk and soap into the concentration camp villages than to continue the extermination bombing—and more human! In practice they did both and U.S. military spending grew year by year. Cultivation of rice and other food crops was discouraged, or strictly controlled, in the Vientiane-held areas because of the official fear that a portion might be reaching the Pathet Lao. Obviously, crops in the Pathet Lao areas were primary targets for toxic defoliants, supplemented by napalm in the harvest season.

It was all done under the charitable title of the "Rural Development Program"—needless to say entirely U.S.-financed—as benevolent a project as herding the survivors from extermination wars against the Red Indians into "reservations." And just as such reservations in the United States are now highlight attractions for tourists, so the plan includes a "model" restoration zone covering the whole of

*On March 16, 1968 (only revealed more than a year later), in the hamlet of Mylai 4, village of Songmy, a company of U.S. infantry massacred some 400 Vietnamese civilians in cold blood.

Vientiane province to impress high level tourists, such as visiting congressmen and Joe Alsop-type journalists that all is well in the CIA-run Land of the Laos.

Aid to the Meos and other unfortunate inmates of the concentration camp villages comes from AID (Agency for International Development), a typically innocuous title for the nefarious nature of its CIA-sponsored activities, at least as far as Laos is concerned. By what means, other than bombs and napalm, entire Meo clans could have been induced to move off their mountain tops and come down to refugee centers in the stuffy plains, is not yet entirely clear. Destruction of their cattle, maize and opium crops must have played a considerable role. It is not an accident that the most intensive use of defoliants has been against villages on the summits and slopes of the areas bordering Vientiane and Xieng Khouang provinces where live the highest concentration of Meos. It is not in character with the Meos to come down into the plains where they can hardly breathe the stuffy humid air. Either is it explicable by even the most lavish bribes that AID could offer.

In some cases I heard of, it was done by trickery; a whole village evacuated on the pretext that it was to be settled on another safer, more fertile mountain top; the women, children and old folk dumped "temporarily" in a refuge center on the plains while the younger men were taken to "inspect the new site." In fact they soon found themselves in military training centers in Thailand and if their families ever saw them again they would be lucky. The Meo villages are virtually inaccessible except for helicopters so the Meos had to be brought down to the plains by terror or trickery. Traditionally the men rarely leave the pure, clear air of the mountain tops, leaving it to their women to descend to the markets in the plains once or twice a month to exchange opium for their simple needs in consumer goods.

In the meantime, U.S. involvement had quietly but dramatically increased. In 1959, Pathet Lao sources put at 300 the number of U.S. military advisers and other personnel in Laos. At the time of the 1962 Geneva Agreements, the figure given for the purposes of "evacuation" of foreign military personnel according to the Agreements was 666, probably less than the real number. Many of them put on civilian clothes and returned as AID or Embassy personnel.

By early 1966, again according to Pathet Lao sources—and they had every possibility to be well informed—there were over 5,000 Americans in Laos, of whom 3,500 were military "advisers" and instructors. After an on-the-spot check, the French journalist Bernard Couret, then writing for *Le Monde Diplomatique* (Paris), informed the Bertrand Russell International War Crimes Tribunal (at Roskilde, Denmark, between November 20 and December 1, 1967) that there were 12,000 Americans, not including families, in Laos. They included instructors and advisers, air crews and ground staff, an army of technicians for road and bridge maintenance and for servicing the incredible total of 100 air strips in Laos, 30 of which were behind the Pathet Lao lines. He included a figure of 500 pilots and crewmen for the CIA-run Air America and Continental Service airlines.

In a special communique on July 20, 1969 to mark the seventh anniversary of the 1962 Geneva Agreements, the Central Committee of the Neo Lao Haksat also gave the figure of 12,000 Americans in Laos, the overwhelming majority of them military "advisors" and "instructors." If one adds to these another 1,000 at the Green Beret HQ 333 at Oudon and a few more hundreds at the Lopbury commando training center (both in Thailand) one has some idea of the extent to which the Pentagon was involved in its secret war in Laos by 1969.

Premier Souvanna Phouma pretended to know nothing about it. Only in 1968 did he finally admit that U.S. planes were in fact bombing Laos. Until then he had contributed to the official myth that they were only on "reconnaissance missions" although he knew perfectly well that the bombings had been going on for four years, since May 1964 to be exact. In October 1969, Souvanna Phouma blandly informed the UN that there were neither U.S. nor Thai troops in Laos, only North Vietnamese. A few weeks later the U.S. Senate inquiry, referred to earlier, summoned CIA director Richard Helms and three military attachés of the U.S. Embassy in Vientiane to explain just what the United States and CIA were up to in Laos.

"It is likely," wrote *New York Times* Washington correspondent, Bernard Lossiter (as reported in the *International Herald Tribune*, October 20, 1969), "that Mr. Helms will be asked about a reported 300 CIA agents said to be operating in the Laotian war. Many are reported to be former Green Berets, recruited to lead Laotian units on reconnaissance missions and terrorist raids. Soldiers and supplies for the war are carried in Air America and Continental Air Service. The two airlines are said to be CIA-operated. The three attachés recalled from Vientiane to testify before the Senate are expected to describe the tactical bombing and ground operations that the American military in Laos reportedly directs for the royal government. There have been reports that every operation now mounted by the royal Lao forces is directed and controlled by the American military establishment there. The U.S. Air Force reportedly flies up to 300 sorties a day against the Pathet Lao and North Vietnamese. On the ground, American captains and majors are said to draw up battle plans in the field and even accompany Laotian units into action."

When the time came for the U.S. ambassador to Thailand, Mr. Leonard Unger, to give evidence before this same inquiry, the *New York Times* reported (*ibid.*, November 27, 1969) that "he refused to testify on what were described as 'six or eight' questions concerning U.S. intelligence commitments in Thailand. One of these concerned the amount of money the United States was paying the Thais for their operations in neutral Laos."

For Souvanna Phouma to deny U.S. and Thai intervention was on precisely the same level as "President" Nguyen Van Thieu's denial that any massacre took place at Songmy at a time when GIs were falling over each other to give the details and the U.S. Army had already placed one of the officers responsible under arrest. Phouma was never very fortunate with his cover-up denials, being continually let down by those he wished to protect. On November 20, 1969 the U.S. Defense Department disclosed that 160 Americans were "missing and two are presumed captured" in Laos.

Despite the enormous effort and investment in dollars and military equipment, the Pentagon could not record any progress on the battlefront during the last months of 1968 and the first half of 1969. Not only had repeated attacks into the Pathet Lao areas been repulsed with heavy losses, but three important strategic bases deep behind the Pathet Lao lines had been lost, airfields and all. They included the big mountain-top base of Pha Thi, another at Nakhang, and the Special Forces and Thai artillery base, a big complex entirely under U.S. and Thai command, at Muong Soui. The latter was an especially embarrassing defeat—the Americans managing to evacuate U.S. and Thai personnel in time to avoid an international scandal, but at the cost of large quantities of artillery and other equipment abandoned. The Muong Soui airfield, also abandoned, was a key center for supplying Meo-manned Special Forces outposts. Other bases of lesser importance were also knocked out in the first half of 1969 together with scores of smaller air-supplied outposts. By July there were only two U.S.-Vientiane bases of any size left behind the Pathet Lao lines, the most important being the Long Cheng-Sam Thong complex south of the Plain of Jars.

The Pathet Lao High Command claimed that 500 planes and helicopters were knocked out or destroyed on the ground in these actions and that their forces took a heavy toll of parachutist, commando and other so-called elite units of the Royal Laotian Army, as well as of the main Special Forces units operating behind their lines. Four regimental commanders were among the slain. It is worth noting that all the fighting at Pathet Lao initiative took place well on their side of the de facto line of partition which Hilsman recognizes the Pathet Lao respected (p. 527).

Early in the second half of 1969 the secret army of General Vang Pao, described in an earlier chapter, was ready to make its debut. It had been built up to about 17,000 regulars in battalion-sized units, supplemented by about another 30,000 irregular semi-commando, semi-bandit units. Some of the latter were kept at Long Cheng for hit-and-run operations, others lived permanently behind the Pathet Lao lines supplied by air drops of opium and munitions. The regular units were essentially shock troops, to be used like the U.S. Marines to spearhead attacks, seize positions and hold them long enough for the regular Laotian army to take over.

In July 1969, U.S. planes intensified their attacks against the towns and villages in and around the Plain of Jars, reducing every building down to the humblest bamboo hut to ashes. The code name in Laotian for this air offensive was "Ke Kheu" (Revenge). In attacks of unprecedented violence, operating out of bases in Thailand, the planes attacked everything that lived, moved, grew or had been made by the hands of man. Schools, hospitals, pagodas, houses, crops ready for harvesting, peasants in the fields, fishermen on the rivers—all were prime targets for "Operation Revenge."

In the successful offensive against the Plain of Jars in mid-August, a new element was introduced in the Laotian war, the use of paratroopers and scores of helicopters to land Vang Pao's Special Forces battalions right onto the Plain. Of the 23 battalions taking part, 16 were Vang Pao troops under direct U.S. command, acting as the vanguard shock troops in the same "kill all, burn all, destroy all" tactics used in South Vietnam. The code name for this action was "Kou Kiêt" (Save Honor).

As it was the height of the rainy season, the Plain of Jars was only thinly defended, the Pathet Lao troops as usual taking advantage of the seasonal operational lull to withdraw to their jungle bases for study courses. Stunned by the violence of the bombing which preceded the offensive, the massive use of paratroopers and heliborne troops, and the huge scale—by Laotian standards—of the operation, the local self-defense forces were no match for the well-trained Vang

Pao mercenaries and their M-16's. Normally the Pathet Lao is well-informed of preparations for an offensive, but this time the enemy's operational headquarters was at Oudon in Thailand, with Long Cheng as the advance base once the offensive got under way. By the time the intensified air shuttle service between Oudon and Long Cheng had signaled what was in the wind it was too late to move regular troops in the required number back into the Plain. Behind Vang Pao's mercenaries, Vientiane and Thai troops moved in to do the "mopping up" and herd the traumatized survivors of the extermination battalions into concentration camp compounds to be exhibited to journalists as "refugees from Pathet Lao terror."

In talks with leading Pathet Lao officals in the North Vietnam-Laotian border areas less than a month after Vang Pao's troops had seized the Plain, I was told that the Pathet Lao forces could and would retake it when the dry season arrived. And in Vientiane a few days later, I was informed that even in Prince Souvanna Phouma's entourage there was considerable nervousness as to the repercussions of the CIA-Vang Pao "notable victory."

The dry season starts about the end of November. By mid-January 1970, two things were happening. Pathet Lao preparations for a counter-offensive could be noted. Vang Pao's Meo mercenaries had no stomach for their role as garrison troops on the Plain; they wanted to get back to their mountains. The regular Vientiane troops were showing no great speed in taking over that very dangerous bit of real estate that the Plain was sure to become. By the end of January, the writing was on the wall. On February 3, Premier Souvanna Phouma proposed the "neutralization" of the Plain of Jars. Strange that he had not thought of that when he was in a "victor" position over four months earlier! The Pathet Lao rejected this, no doubt having in mind their previous experiences with "neutralization."

On February 5, the CIA started flying out in C-130 planes some 23,000 unfortunate civilians from the concentration camp villages they had set up in the Sam Thong-Long Cheng area. Synthetically created flotsam, they had to be removed so the Pathet Lao "fish" would find no "sea" to move around in. Also it would ease the U.S. conscience to know that those who would now be bombed were only the "naughty ones" who had avoided concentration or had escaped from the camps.

As the Pathet Lao—by then described as "North Vietnamese" troops—predictably closed in, the Vientiane troops predictably moved out. This is no reflection on their courage or fighting capacity, but on their realism and in many cases their patriotism. That they rarely stand and fight the Pathet Lao is their affirmation of refusing to kill and be killed to implement what are so obviously U.S. policies against their own national interests. If this had not been clear enough before it certainly became obvious during the previous twelve months as they saw U.S. air power blasting their whole country to pieces.

On February 13, after having claimed another "victory" the previous day, Vientiane announced the loss of 12 key hill positions, vital approaches guarding the Plain. Vientiane losses were given as 19 killed and 50 wounded which does not suggest any very enthusiastic resistance. The following day it was announced that heavy artillery was being flown out of the Plain and that the latter was being prepared "as a trap to lure the North Vietnamese and crush them by air power." On February 16, it was announced from Saigon that 400 fighter-bombers were attacking "North Vietnamese troops, trucks and supply lines in Laos" and the following day B-52 operations in South Vietnam were switched to Laos. The newspaper headlines made it appear as if this deployment of U.S. strategic and tactical air power in Laos was something new. In fact it had been going on for years and B-52's had been regularly used in Laos for at least a year. Tucked away in a UPI story from Saigon on February 16 was the confirmation that: "B-52's and a fleet of 400 fighter-bombers have been flying daily missions into Laos for months. But the new emergency strikes, requiring all the planes available, underscored the urgency of the situation in

Laos." At 3 a.m. on the morning of February 21, despite the bombings, Pathet Lao forces launched their final assault and the Plain of Jars was firmly in their hands within a matter of hours.

In an ironic commentary on February 23 on the recapture of the Plain, *Le Figaro* (Paris' leading daily paper and far removed from any suspicion of left-wing sympathies) wrote: "How many men were thrown into the decisive offensive on Saturday morning? In Vientiane sometimes they speak of 6,000 troops, sometimes 400. It is said that the battle was a tough one . . . also that there was practically no fight at all. Among the considered opinions offered, one hears that government troops suffered heavy losses—also that losses were very light. We heard of a rout, the desperate flight of the 1,400 defenders of Xieng Khouang, described as lost in the hills or hiding out in the beds of rivers which crisscross the Plain. Now, it is said that the evacuation, prepared in advance, took place as scheduled."

Again the cry went up that North Vietnamese troops were involved to bolster the old charge of North Vietnamese "aggression" in Laos. At the time of writing I have no information one way or the other. But I do recall that on two other major crises over Laos when the same charges were made, they proved to be false (the seizure of the Plain of Jars on January 1, 1961 by troops of Kong Le and the Pathet Lao and the battle of Nam Tha in May 1962, both dealt with in an earlier chapter). Therefore reports about North Vietnamese troops at the Plain of Jars and related actions in 1970 should be treated with the greatest reserve. In any case the Pathet Lao forces, veterans of nearly 25 years of jungle warfare and during that period having grown and developed in every respect, are absolutely capable of waging such actions on their own. In all battles against the Vientiane troops, including those in which there was not the faintest possibility of North Vietnamese support, they have come off the victors, even under what appeared to be impossible conditions.

President Nixon acted as predictably as did the Vientiane

troops when the Pathet Lao forces continued to advance. First, he denied that any U.S. forces were involved; then he sent letters to premiers Harold Wilson and Alexei Kosygin on March 5, asking them to use their influence to move the situation from the battlefield to the conference table. Just as in the weeks preceding the Nam Tha battle, President Kennedy was quite happy with the situation as long as Nosavan's forces were advancing, but demanded a conference as soon as the tables were turned, so now too President Nixon demanded a conference only when faced with a defeat. It was not surprising that Kosygin coldly rebuffed the demand and advised Nixon to stop the bombings and get out of Laos.

It was about this time that the situation in Laos began to blow up in the United States—not because there was much editorial indignation about the morality of the U.S. presence there, but because things had gone wrong. Official Washington's lies about Laos started flying home to roost. "No Americans stationed in Laos have ever been killed in ground action," said President Nixon on March 5, in the same statement in which he had appealed to Wilson and Kosygin for a conference (while still refusing publication of the transcript of the Senate's sub-committee inquiry into American involvement in Laos). Next day came news that a Captain Joseph Bush had been killed on February 10, 1969 helping protect a "secret" U.S. base at Muong Sai, 20-odd miles west of the Plain of Jars. His wife supplied the evidence. The White House then announced that six civilians, apart from Captain Bush, had also been killed. Within a few days the figure had reached 27. On March 10, the father of Captain Bush revealed an interesting detail: "a government-supplied tombstone had an inscription saying that his son had died in Vietnam." This raised the tantalizing question as to how many other Americans officially "killed in action in South Vietnam" had in fact died in America's secret war in Laos.

On the same day it was also revealed that for more than four years American military personnel serving in Laos were receiving extra "hostile fire pay" of $65 a month and pilots flying across Laos to bomb North or South Vietnam from bases in Thailand also received extra bonuses. About the same time, Senator Stuart Symington, who had chaired the Senate sub-committee whose transcript of evidence was then still suppressed, asserted that casualties of American airmen "far exceeded the 27 Americans that the administration acknowledged have been killed or were missing in ground operations in Laos." Figures of up to 400 airmen were being cited. Washington *Post* correspondent T. D. Allman revealed (March 17) that "more than a dozen Americans were killed in Laos two years ago in defense of a secret American installation which assisted U.S. bombings of North Vietnam. The incident, until now kept secret, was not included in President Nixon's (March 6) speech and it has had an important effect on North Vietnamese strategy in northeast Laos." Senator Symington weighed in with the charge that testimony regarding this incident had been censored out of his sub-committee's report. The base referred to was at Pha Thi which was eliminated by the Pathet Lao in 1968. Allman correctly describes it as "an American radar reconnaissance and rescue base in extreme northeastern Laos which guided U.S. aircraft to their targets and electronically released their bomb loads by radio impulse."

As an installation on Laotian territory, directing bombing attacks on targets in North Vietnam, the latter had every right under international rules of war to go in and try to knock it out. Furthermore, as 80 per cent of the bombing attacks against the North were flown across Laotian air space from Thailand, North Vietnam also had every right to traverse Laotian ground space to get at those bases in Thailand and try to destroy them. Pha Thi was the most important of such radar bases but only one of many, the operation of which amounted to acts of war against North Vietnam on the part of the Vientiane government.

These revelations began to put Nixon in the same position as the late President Eisenhower when he denied there had been any U-2 flights over the Soviet Union at a moment when U-2 pilot, Gary Powers, was in Soviet hands.

Then there was the question of American personnel in Laos. After persistent probing and denials that there were any "ground combat personnel," the State Department had admitted on September 24, 1969 that there were "about 500 U.S. Government personnel in Laos, plus 330 aid contract personnel." On March 6, President Nixon upped this figure to 1,040 of whom 616 were "government personnel—engaged either in military advisory or training capacities." This came close to the 616 given by the United States at the time of the 1962 Geneva Conference, who were all supposed to have been withdrawn. It of course excluded an unknown number in the thousands who could be switched from South Vietnam and Thailand on tactical operations as the occasion demanded.

As to the AID personnel, there were some interesting revelations about that also. "The U.S. civilian AID mission in Laos is being used as a cover for CIA agents in clandestine operations against the Communist enemy," writes correspondent Jack Foisie in the Los Angeles *Times* (March 11). "Agents posing as members for the U.S. Agency for International Development (AID) mission's Rural Development Division are recruiting and training pro-government guerrillas to fight Communists, detect enemy movements deep in their own territory and act as ground controllers for aircraft. . . . Conversations with people throughout Laos in the past several weeks indicate that the number of agents posing as civilian AID workers totals several hundred."

Foisie goes on to describe other disguises adopted by the CIA for its various innocent-sounding agencies: "The Rural Development Annex appears to be the successor to 'White Star', the code name under which CIA activity in Laos was originally conducted. Although nominally under control of the AID mission director, Charles Mann, annex people answer only to the CIA chief in Laos. There is another secret organization hidden within the AID mission compound. It is called the Special Requirements Office, and its personnel provide supplies for the clandestine units. . . . Many members of the annex are former American servicemen who fought in Vietnam. Often they come from the Special Forces and their job in Laos is about the same—without the green beret."

How right the Laotian people are to mistrust such foreign missions, no matter how innocent and high-sounding their names! "Conspiracy" is hardly a misnomer for such double-dealing toward both the Laotian and American people. One of the most alarming aspects is that none of this skulduggery would have come out in the American press had it not been for the crisis over the Plain of Jars.

Three journalists, two Americans from the *New York Times* and *Life Magazine* and one Frenchman from Agence France Presse, managed to get inside the no-longer-so-secret CIA base at Long Cheng. They were able to slip in unnoticed but were later arrested by a Laotian colonel, interrogated by an American "in civilian clothes—presumably CIA—and hustled out at U.S. Embassy direction on a plane bound for the capital of Vientiane," according to a report in the Washington *Post* (February 26). U.S. Ambassador Godley was quoted as saying he "had lost all interest in the press" after the incident.

T. D. Allman, quoted earlier, was one of the three journalists who penetrated Long Cheng. He describes it *(New York Times*, March 6, 1970) as "the center of operations of the U.S. military and the Central Intelligence Agency in Northeastern Laos." He refers to U.S. military men clad in civilian clothes "riding in open Jeeps and carrying M-16 rifles and hand guns. These young Americans," explains Allman, "are mostly ex-Green Berets, hired on CIA contract to advise and train Laotian troops. The fact that they are temporarily CIA personnel and no longer connected with their Army units allows the U.S. government to say that it has no soldiers fighting in Laos."

"Nearly every male between the ages of 12 and 50 is in the army organized by the CIA and headed by Maj. Gen. Vang Pao," Allman continues. "The others—women, old men and children—have been resettled in formerly unpopulated hills south and west of Long Cheng. They are almost totally dependent on U.S. gifts of rice, medicine and clothing. Gen. Vang Pao's army, despite heavy U.S. support, has not fared well. His guerrilla forces which once numbered about 18,000 men, now total about 6,000. But they have been augmented by reinforcements from the regular Laotian Army units so that he has a total of about 12,000 men under his command." Allman estimated that planes landed at the Long Cheng airport at the rate of about one per minute.

At Vientiane airport in October 1969, I estimated the CIA-run Air America and Continental Air Services planes interspersed with T-28 fighter-bombers were taking off at the rate of about one every two minutes on supply and bombing operations.

Henry Kamm of the *New York Times*, now something of an expert on recent developments in Laos, writing in the *International Herald Tribune* (March 23), refers to the further weakening of the Vientiane government's positions because of "mounting indications that its best fighting force, the clandestine American-backed army of Gen. Vang Pao, is at a low ebb. Sam Thong, one of the government's two principle bases in northern Laos, had to be rapidly evacuated. The second base, Long Cheng was endangered. The low morale of the general and his man-and-boy soldiers were plainly in evidence."

One more American "strong man" in Southeast Asia on his way out and one more CIA "Bay of Pigs" type of disaster; thousands of Laotians killed and wounded, tens of thousands more made homeless as a result of U.S. policies which are a total negation of self-determination.

There is a puzzling aspect of the most recent debacle in Laos: Why did the CIA launch the September 1969 action against the Plain of Jars? A tempting hypothesis is that it was not really intended as a military success at all. Rather, the CIA meant to create a certain situation rather than a solid military success. It occurred at a time when pressure was building up in the press and Congress to curtail U.S. engagements in Laos. The Pentagon and the CIA must have known, should have known at least, that the Plain would be retaken and the atmosphere of crisis built up, just as in fact did happen. Was it Nixon's way of forcing the hands of Congress, or the CIA-Pentagon's way of forcing the hand of

Nixon himself to halt disengagement in Southeast Asia by proving the necessity for continuing U.S. military presence into the foreseeable future? If the commitment is to be reduced in one area it must be increased in another. Dominos that had refused to show any sign of falling were to be shaken hard by U.S. policies until they really did start to totter. What happened over the border in Cambodia at the height of the Laotian crisis provides food for thought along these lines.

Some normally well-informed contacts in Washington have advanced a more dismal explanation which, if true, would show that the CIA is even more out of touch with realities in Laos than it was in South Vietnam on the eve of the Tet offensive. Nixon, they say, has been persuaded that things are really going well in South Vietnam; "Vietnamization" is going to work, the NLF is once again "at the end of its tether." Withdrawals can go ahead in a leisurely fashion without disturbing the relation of forces; the Thieu-Ky regime can be maintained. The only thing is to make sure that the perimeter countries, Laos and Cambodia, are not endangered by the gradual reduction of U.S. forces in Vietnam. Nixon, according to this hypothesis, was persuaded that the September operation was "sound" militarily and American control of the Plain of Jars would guarantee no further left-wing trouble in Laos, or "Communist penetration" from the North, just as the toppling of Sihanouk would end the risk of further cooperation between Cambodia, North Vietnam and the Provisional Revolutionary Government in the South. Once the situations in Laos and Cambodia had been stabilized, withdrawals of U.S. troops from Vietnam could go ahead even faster and Nixon could go on to win the mid-term elections on the strength of establishing a "Pax Americana" in Southeast Asia.

Evidently Nixon, convinced by the Pentagon advisers that the adventures in Laos and Cambodia would bring military victory within his grasp, expected the negotiators of North Vietnam and the South Vietnam Provisional Revolutionary government to be so demoralized by his impending "victory" that they would accept the "generous" surrender terms he was prepared to send to the Paris conference, along with a new chief of the U.S. delegation. To emphasize what he thought was his new position of strength, he sent over 100 bombers on successive days deep into North Vietnamese territory in the most flagrant violation of the agreements reached in Paris.

All these illusions were certain, like "Vietnamization," to blow up in the President's face long before the mid-term elections in November 1970, as already indicated by the reverses in Laos and by the catastrophic consequences of the invasion of Cambodia.

There have been all sorts of direful predictions that the Pathet Lao would sweep on to take Luang Prabang—as it is generally conceded they could easily do, probably Vientiane as well. Until now the Pathet Lao forces have always shown themselves modest at the moment of victory. A notable case in point was Nam Tha in 1962 when all observers agree they could have swept on to occupy the left bank of the Mekong and exterminated the fleeing rightist troops. They made no attempt to do either. Instead they agreed to sit in on the Geneva Conference in which the United States suddenly discovered great interest. Similarly, after retaking the Plain of Jars, the Pathet Lao leadership proposed on March 6 a five-point plan to bring peace to Laos, based on the essence of the 1962 Geneva Agreements, as follows:

(1) The United States must withdraw completely from Laos and cease its military activities in the country.

(2) In accordance with the 1962 Geneva Agreements, Laos must refrain from any military alliances with other countries.

(3) An election should be held for a new National Assembly to form a democratic government.

(4) During an interim period, the Laotian political parties should set up a consultative conference and a coalition government. The parties should agree on the establish-

ment of a security zone to ensure the unhindered functioning of the parties.

(5) The Laotian problem must be settled by the parties concerned.

This was not presented on a "take it or leave it" basis, but as a basis for discussion. Premier Souvanna Phouma's first response to the peace plan was considerably warmer than Washington's, but the latter's sour reaction was a sure pointer to the line Souvanna Phouma would eventually follow. For internal reasons, he seemed to be interested in preliminary talks and a special Pathet Lao envoy came to Vientiane to present the plan officially.

The five-point plan might have been the basis for restoring national unity in Laos, and providing a political solution which could in turn have pointed the way toward a political settlement in Vietnam. But in the meantime Washington thought it had counteracted its defeat in Laos with a "victory" in overthrowing Prince Sihanouk in Cambodia. This chance, perhaps the last, for a negotiated settlement in Laos was rejected by Souvanna Phouma's government on April 1, on the ground that the demand for a halt to U.S. bombings as a precondition for talks was "unacceptable."

With the rejection of the peace plan and the new situation in Cambodia, the Pathet Lao went into action again, this time in the Bolovens Plateau area of the "three frontiers region" where South Vietnam, Cambodia and Laos meet. The province of Attopeu, including the provincial capital of the same name, was liberated quickly. Attopeu was an important base for the rightist forces and the main entry point for the clandestine Special Forces which the Americans were running into Laos from South Vietnam. Its loss was a severe blow against all American operations in that part of southern Laos. There was more to come as the Pathet Lao went on to encircle Saravane, some 60 miles to the north of Attopeu, knocking out a number of U.S.-supplied hilltop bases as they went. In the North, Pathet Lao troops pushed forward to the

Thai frontier in several places, beating back counter-offensive operations in the northern and southern sectors. At the same time they tightened their encirclement of the only two important U.S. bases behind their lines, at Sam Thong and Long Cheng. Several times Pathet Lao commandos penetrated the perimeter of these bases to shell Vang Pao's headquarters. In one such operation, it was reported, Vang Pao was wounded and flown out to Oudon in Thailand for hospitalization.

By the end of April, hundreds of the Vang Pao mercenaries had deserted and were passed back through Pathet Lao territory to their native villages. In the three months since the Plain of Jars was retaken by the Pathet Lao, at least half of Vang Pao's forces were wiped out. To fill the gap, the Americans started bringing in Special Forces from South Vietnam—another secret kept from the public but which was leaked by the Saigon Foreign Minister Tran Van Lam at the Djakarta conference on Cambodia on May 17 and reluctantly confirmed the following day by U.S. Defense Secretary Laird. According to Pathet Lao sources, 2,000 more Special Forces troops were in a crash training program in Thailand, to be rushed to the rescue of the badly shattered and demoralized Vang Pao remnants.

By the end of May at least 5,000 Thai troops were fighting in Laos and more were being sent to be "integrated" with the regular Vientiane army units. The U.S. command hoped to avoid a complete military collapse in Laos by throwing in more Special Forces and Thai troops, together with the use of improved weapons and increased air power.

As for the Laotian resistance forces, their leadership obviously was thinking of the new military perspectives arising from the fact that Laos had become an integral part of the Second Indochina War. In mid-May in Hanoi, I met Oun Heuan Phounsavath who was attending the Summit Conference of the Peoples of Indochina as a member of the Neo Lao Haksat delegation. I asked for his estimate of the Conference.

"In the immediate future," he said, "the results of the Conference will prove to have raised the combativity of the

Indochina peoples to a new, high level. Until now the U.S. imperialists abrogated to themselves the right of waging a single war against the peoples of Indochina. In reality, they forged the unity of our three peoples. This will be demonstrated in concrete actions in the months and years to come. . . . Each of our three countries has its own position based on the realities of each country. We respect each other's positions. The Summit Conference absorbed these viewpoints, the synthesis of which is reflected in the communique."

Obviously, this will be expressed in the military-political events of the Second Indochina War and in the nature of future relations among the nations of Indochina after their final victory. One thing sèems certain—just as there is now a single Indochina war, there can be only a single Indochina peace.

8

Double Standards, Double Dealing

Washington's official pretext for the gradual escalation from interference to intervention, then downright aggression against the Laotian people has always been related to North Vietnamese "intervention" or "aggression." In fact, Hanoi's policy strictly has been to let the Laotians settle their own affairs. Without U.S. interference, the Laotians would have settled their affairs in a manner satisfactory to themselves and the North Vietnamese. The Vietnam of Ho Chi Minh had no intention, and little interest, in seeking to impose a communist or pro-communist regime on Laos, even if it ever had the means to do so. As far as the 1954 Geneva Agreements on Laos and Cambodia were concerned, Hanoi's leaders were perfectly satisfied with the letter and the spirit of these agreements, the essence of which was that Laos and Cambodia would become neutral buffer states between Vietnam and other states of mainland Southeast Asia. This was the essential element in the meeting of East-West minds at Geneva.

For the British and French, the buffer state concept quieted their anxieties regarding an expansion, or at least a too rapid expansion, beyond the confines of Vietnam of "communist ideas" with which they identified the Vietminh. The Cambodian-Lao *cordon sanitaire* would protect their sphere of interest in Thailand, Malaya and other areas from the "red virus." Vietnam could not be saved—the Vietminh had won—but ideologically it could be amputated from the rest of Southeast Asia, and if it buttoned itself on to

China—already "lost"—this was an acceptable price to pay for its isolation elsewhere. Meanwhile SEATO could provide a military shield of protection for the states on the other side of the buffer.

For Hanoi, with a South Vietnam to be reunified by elections within two years (as the Geneva Agreements provided), the sea to the East and South, neutral buffer states in the West and fraternal, socialist People's China in the North, they could go ahead in peace and independence and build up a democratic, socialist state which would prove a still more irresistible attraction to the compatriots in the South when the time for elections arrived. It was in this spirit that agreement could be reached at Geneva on the future status of Laos and Cambodia.

Laos was in a very different state of social-political evolution than Vietnam. Its revolution would find its own tempo. If there were Vietminh troops there during the anti-French war, this was on a friendly, mutual-help basis, forged by the resistance forces of Indochina to coordinate their common efforts to defeat French colonialism and bring peace and independence to each of the component parts. They resisted French efforts to buy off each of them separately in order to crush them separately once the colonialist forces were strong enough.

The Vietminh forces in Laos withdrew after the 1954 Geneva Agreements to the unanimous satisfaction of the International Control Commission which supervised their departure. They had no thoughts of ever returning. Their comrades-in-arms, the Pathet Lao, had broad popular support, including the powerful Buddhist clergy on the one hand and the nationalist-neutralist forces on the other, together representing all that there was of organized public opinion in the country. Laotian political leaders should be able to agree on common programs; there would be no major problems in effecting national reconciliation. Nor would the risk arise that a government resulting from this national reconciliation might adopt policies representing any threat or danger to an independent Vietnam.

Busy as they were healing the ravages of war, bringing about unity in the North and preparing for the nationwide elections, the last thing the Hanoi leaders wanted was a Laotian problem on their hands. The Geneva Agreements seemed a sure guarantee.

But the United States of Eisenhower and Dulles, before the Geneva Agreements were even signed, had decided to move into Laos, indirectly if possible through stooges such as Katay and Sananikone, directly if that did not work. This policy was continued by the administrations of Kennedy and Johnson, and is continued today by Nixon. Whatever help North Vietnam, at any particular stage, gave the patriotic forces in Laos was entirely a reaction to United States intervention. North Vietnam alone or together with People's China, supported by the Soviet Union (as Co-Chairman of the Geneva Conference), took innumerable initiatives to bring the Laotian question back onto the rails of the Geneva Agreements, to reinforce the supervisory role of the ICC. They denounced Sananikone's closing down of the ICC and his repudiation of the Geneva Agreements. They demanded ICC investigation of wholesale breaches of the Agreements and had nothing to fear from investigations of charges of Vietnamese intervention. For two years during which U.S. intervention increased, the British government turned a deaf ear to North Vietnamese requests, relayed by the Soviet government, to revive the ICC. The British acted only when it would serve the interests of the United States and its stooges in Laos. When North Vietnam did start sending substantial aid to Laos, this was at the specific request of the legal government of Souvanna Phouma, at a time when he needed the support of the Pathet Lao for his own political and physical survival.

Hanoi maintained a similar, consistent attitude toward South Vietnam. As long as the United States kept out of the South physically, and in fact long after there was physical United States intervention, Hanoi let the South Vietnamese people try and settle their own affairs, despite the perfidious tearing up of the Geneva Agreements, the repudiation of the

Geneva pledge of general elections in July 1956 to unify the country, and the savage repression, amounting to attempted extermination, of the members and supporters of the independence struggle. Hilsman recognizes that it was only long after U.S. intervention began in the South, that the North really started to help the resistance movement there.*

As far as Laos is concerned, obviously Hanoi was not going to sit idly by and see its former comrades-in-arms across the frontier exterminated so that the United States could take over from the defeated French as the new colonial power. If at some stage the North Vietnamese helped the Laotian patriotic forces repel U.S. intervention, most fair-minded persons even with a minimum knowledge of the background would applaud. In doing so the North Vietnamese would be defending the interests of the Laotian people and of peace in Southeast Asia. They would be acting in the spirit of the 1951 alliance between the resistance forces of the three states of Indochina, and of the Conference of the Peoples of Indochina in Phnom Penh, May 1965, pledging common action against U.S. aggression if further attacks were made upon the participating countries.

History would in fact judge the North Vietnamese harshly had they turned their back on their former Laotian allies and their compatriots in the South in their hour of direst need. The North Vietnamese leaders had to make their decisions in the light of national interests—certainly threatened if U.S. military presence was installed along her frontiers—and the international situation, particularly North Vietnam's position

*Referring to the State Department's White Paper on "Aggression from the North," used to justify the start of the American bombing of North Vietnam, Hilsman comments (p. 531): "No captured documents, equipment, or materials were presented that indicate either the presence of North Vietnamese regular units or of individual North Vietnamese in significant numbers. The white paper was able to present the case studies of only four captured infiltrators who were ethnic North Vietnamese. No evidence was presented of the presence of regular North Vietnamese units except the allegations of two of these and two other captured Vietcong of southern origin." Hilsman who knew very well the methods used to extract such allegations, does not set much store on them.

as a member of the socialist camp. Participants in the 1957 conference in Moscow of world communist parties had agreed that while they were against the export of revolution, they were also against the export of counter-revolution. They pledged to mobilize their resources, including the military resources of countries where communist parties held state power, to help people and countries which had risen up in revolution and were victims of international support of counter-revolution.

Thus, in relation to her position within the international communist movement and the socialist camp, the Democratic Republic of Vietnam would be fulfilling her international obligations in helping the Pathet Lao defeat U.S.-sponsored counter-revolution in Laos.

There were other factors. By 1965, the United States had created one single military front against the peoples of Indochina. It took the form of U.S. combat troops against the people of the South; the air war against the North of Vietnam; "special war" in Laos; threats to invade Cambodia coupled with bombing and shelling of the latter's frontier villages. These were all part of a single, coordinated front. But while the United States reserved to itself the privilege of waging one single war, as did the French in their time, the victims were supposed to wait boxed up in their respective pens to be butchered one by one. Can anyone blame them if they broke out to unite and help each other?

Eighty per cent of air attacks against North Vietnam were being flown from bases in Thailand across Laotian air space, guided to their targets by American-manned radar bases in Laos, the bombs actually dropped by electronic signals from these bases. If the United States had the right to use Laotian air space to attack North Vietnam, did not the North Vietnamese have the right to cross Laotian ground space to hit back at the bases in Thailand—not to mention the right of entering Laotian territory to wipe out the radar bases? Had Prince Souvanna Phouma cared a fig to preserve Laotian neutrality he would have denied the use of Laotian air space to attack a neighboring country; as it was, he never even raised his voice against it.

Another facet of the double standards Washington uses in its self-imposed role of international gendarme is that the United States reserves to itself the monopoly of using foreign troops in their pay against the Laotian (and South Vietnamese) people. Thai, South Vietnamese, Kuomintang Chinese, Philippine and other mercenaries in Laos (South Korean, Australian, New Zealand, Thai and Philippine troops in South Vietnam). But for the North Vietnamese to help their closest neighbors and compatriots was a "crime" to be punished by extermination—"Let's bomb 'em back to the Stone Age," as General Lemay demanded.

Had the socialist camp reacted similarly, Soviet planes would have been bombing American cities; Soviet and Chinese submarines sinking U.S. supply convoys in the Pacific (thousands and not six or a dozen tons of supplies daily), Chinese, North Korean, Cuban, Hungarian and other troops fighting in South Vietnam and Laos!

At the beginning of 1961 for instance, after Kong Le and Kingkapo had seized the Plain of Jars, Thai troops under U.S. command were parachuted into the area on three successive days, beginning January 1. At that time not even the wildest imagination could conceive a Vietnamese presence, hundreds of miles over trackless jungle-covered mountains from their frontier. Nor could North Vietnamese be associated with any of the major crises which sparked off the Washington exercises in brinkmanship: the defeat of Katay's military campaigns, the affair of the two Pathet Lao battalions, the escape of Souphanouvong, the Kong Le coup, the seizure of the Plain of Jars. The "Ho Chi Minh trail" pretext had not even been invented at that time. But U.S. intervention was apparent for all to see.

Another example of Washington's double standards is that the United States reserves to itself the monopoly of using a country like Thailand for training and operational bases and "attack-free sanctuaries," as a depot from which to transport war supplies for use against neighboring countries, and as territory in which to maneuver troops in its pay and under its command to outflank and attack its victims from the rear. (as in Nosavan's attack on Vientiane, for example). What an outcry there would have been if China had used northern Laos to send military supplies to North Vietnam! Or had invaded Laos and Thailand under the U.S.-invented pretext of "hot pursuit" to destroy the Kuomintang remnants harrassing her frontier areas from bases in those countries!

From the beginning of its intervention in Laos and elsewhere in Indochina, the United States has applied the jungle law of "might is right." Had Hanoi and the Pathet Lao, and countries friendly to them, employed the same official pretexts used by Washington to justify its intervention, U.S. "sanctuaries" in Thailand, Guam, Okinawa and the Philippines would have been bombed for a start. Thailand would have been invaded for committing "acts of war" as defined under international conventions against the Democratic Republics of Vietnam and Laos. In applying its double standards, Washington already had pushed things to the very verge of a widened war in Southeast Asia which only a miracle could avert.

To be sure, the Nixon administration is running into wider and shaper opposition among the American people. In Congress, many liberal lawmakers are horrified at the whittling away of their prerogatives, particularly with respect to the power to make war. This has led to a head-on collision between the President and the Senate over the Cambodian invasion and to an attempt by a group of Senators to pass a measure, much stronger than the resolution on Laos, to curb U.S. intervention in Cambodia. The Cooper-Church resolution, named after the Republican and Democratic senators who drafted it, was aimed at cutting off funds for any U.S. military activities in Cambodia after June 30, 1970—the date at which Nixon had promised to pull out all U.S. combat troops. In its original form the measure also would cut off funds and supplies for other foreign troops operating in Cambodia. At the time of writing, it still remains to be seen whether or not it will suffer the same fate as the resolution on Laos—under cover of curbing the use of U.S. combat troops, allow the President to continue, even intensify, the operations of CIA-sponsored Special Forces and other "hidden warfare," while supporting and directing the invasion of Cambodia by U.S. client states in Southeast Asia.

Long before the June 30 deadline approached, in addition to Saigon troops on the rampage in Cambodia, Thai troops and CIA-organized Special Forces commandos were committed to the defense of Phnom Penh against the Cambodian resistance. There was even talk of using South Korean, Indonesian and Taiwan troops—a sort of international army of counter-revolution, armed and financed by the United States—to "save" Cambodia from the "Vietcong" and the "North Vietnamese." Speculation was rife about a new partitition of Cambodia—South Vietnam from one side and Thailand from the other, the "traditional" enemies of the past—but now both acting as agents and on behalf of the United States.

"The cynicism of the U.S. Executive reached its peak," said Sihanouk in his opening speech at the Summit Conference of the Peoples of Indochina, on April 24, 1970, "when he demanded that the resistance forces of our three countries evacuate their own countries in response to the withdrawal of a part of the U.S. forces, and especially when our resistance [according to him] had become 'foreign intervention' on our own soil. Where then should our liberation armies go? Have the U.S. aggressors through some operation of the Holy Ghost become pure-blooded Indochinese?"

It is clear that U.S. aims to dominate Southeast Asia have not changed one whit. The Indochinese peoples have no alternative but to continue the struggle for full independence. This struggle will be the major factor in Southeast Asia in the decade which has just been ushered in.

Index